T0267286

FLORA AND FAUNA
OF THE BIBLE

A GUIDE FOR BIBLE READERS AND NATURALISTS

FLORA AND FAUNA
OF THE BIBLE
A GUIDE FOR BIBLE READERS AND NATURALISTS

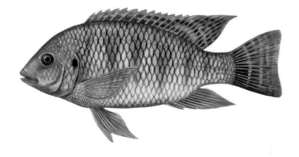

**PETER
GOODFELLOW**

JOHN BEAUFOY PUBLISHING

In memory of my late wife, June,
who was always happy when I was
"scribbling" another manuscript.

Reprinted in 2023

First published in the United Kingdom in 2015 by John Beaufoy Publishing,
11 Blenheim Court, 316 Woodstock Road, Oxford OX2 7NS, England
www.johnbeaufoy.com

10 9 8 7 6 5 4 3 2

ISBN 978-1-913679-55-2

Printed and bound in Malaysia by Times Offset (M) Sdn. Bhd.

Designed and typeset by Gulmohur Press, New Delhi
Project management by Rosemary Wilkinson
Cartography by William Smuts

PAGE 2: OLIVE TREE; PAGE 3: TILAPIA

CONTENTS

"IN THE BEGINNING..."

All good 'Where to watch...' natural history books include descriptions of the landscape where the naturalists should go. Our trip through the Bible needs a few words about our destination, The Holy Land. Not everyone will be able to see the Promised Land at first hand, but some idea of an environment that is so very different from our own and the variety of wildlife which may be seen there will hopefully bring to the fore some memories of species we have seen in the wild or images from books or films, so that the scripture references to cedars or thorns or olives can be part of a real place, not just names on a page.

A glance at a map shows clearly that the wildlife of the Bible is confined in a narrow country in the south-east corner of the Mediterranean Sea. Since ancient times, Palestine (or Canaan, as it was called before that) has been a narrow corridor between the land mass of Arabia and Southeast Asia, and the Mediterranean Sea, which was an ideal route for traders travelling between Egypt and Asia Minor, and for the armies of leaders in the quest to enlarge their empires. It was – and is – a territory that was often fought over.

A closer look at the land reveals a markedly north-south orientation of highlands and lowlands, and their related climatic and vegetation zones. Here is a land that varies between the harsh, barren landscape of the south, to the land 'flowing with milk and honey' (Job, ch. 20, v. 17) west of the Jordan, to the majestic Mount Hermon in the north. For most of Palestine, geographers say the area has a Mediterranean climate. There is a marked dry season from mid-June to mid-September. The winter rain is not so regular, and appreciable rainfall may not occur till after Christmas. The summers are hot. Average temperatures in the Jordan valley from May to October are usually well over 30°C/86°F; winters are much cooler, below 10°C/50°F in December to February; in Jerusalem the average August temperature is 29°C/85°F, whereas in January it is only 8°C/47°F. Frost may occur then at night, and even snow may fall in the south, as happened in the winter of 1991–1992 when banana plantations in Jericho were ruined. The temperature and rainfall vary greatly through the area because of the landscape; the western-facing slopes are wetter than the eastern, and temperatures tend to increase the further one goes from the sea and further south.

Many years ago the Psalmist wrote 'the earth is full of your creatures' (Psalm 104, v. 24).

LEBANON

Sayda
JEBEL LIBAN
Jazzin
JEBEL ESH SHARQI
Damascus

Tyre
Mt Hermon▲

Hula Nature Reserve●
El Qunaytirah
SYRIA

Nahariyya
Lake Tiberias
(Sea of Galilee)
GOLAN

'Akko
Capernaum
HEIGHTS

Haifa
Tiberias
Mt Carmel▲

Nazareth
Yarmuk

Afula
Dar'a

Jenin

Hadera
GILEAD

Netanya
Jordan
Ajlun
Mafráq

Tulkarm

Herzliyya
Nablus
Zarqa

Tel Aviv
WEST BANK
Zarqa

Rishon le Zion
Ba'al Hazor▲
Amman

Rehovot
Jericho

Ashdod
Jerusalem

Ashqelon
Madaba

GAZA
Bethlehem

STRIP
Hebron
DEAD SEA

Gaza
Mujib

Khan Yunis
Mazra

Beersheba
Quatrana

ISRAEL

Dimona

Tafila

Negev

EGYPT
JORDAN

Petra

Ma'an

Wadi al Araba

El Kuntilla
ESH SHARA

Yotvata

Jebel Ram▲

Eilat
Aqaba

0   50 miles

0   50 km

Gulf of Aqaba

MEDITERRANEAN

SEA

Wadi el Jeib

TOPOGRAPHICAL MAP OF ISRAEL

ROCKROSE

This was certainly true in biblical times. At the eastern end of the Mediterranean Sea, from Anatolia in southern Turkey to southern Africa, runs the great Rift Valley. Some of the most diverse segments of habitat in it are the plains of Syria, Lebanon, Israel and Jordan, with the green belt of the Jordan River running through. This is the heart of the Holy Land and its flora and fauna. The landscape gave a great variety of habitats, even though the underlying rock was largely limestone or sandstone, except for the alluvial plain and Rift Valley. The lowlands behind the sand dunes of the coast are now orange groves, vineyards, and fields of cereals and vegetables, but in ancient times there would have been large areas of marshland as well as settlements. The hill country still has extensive areas of wild flowers in spring and shrubland of Dwarf Oaks, Carob trees and Rockrose. This scrub can be very dense, particularly around Mount Carmel and on the hills around Galilee. The Rift Valley has vegetation the thickness of jungle and tropical heat in summer to go with it! The heat and the water create a lush, green ribbon of vegetation that closely follows the river, and consists of Tamarisk, which can grow to a height of 15 m (over 45 ft). The small tree

Jerusalem Thorn (*Paliurus spina-christi*), 3–4 m (10–13 ft) tall, is native to the area. Another similarly sized tree, known as Christ's Thorn or Jujube (*Ziziphus spina-christi*), also grows in Israel; its thorns are up to 2 cm (¾ in) long. Both trees have been said to be the one used to make Christ's crown of thorns. Commentators believe the Jujube is the last tree mentioned in Jotham's parable in Judges ch. 9, vv. 8–15 (see Chapter 2, p. 32).

Many waterbirds are still found north of Galilee at the Hula (or Huleh) nature reserve. It is a marsh of papyrus and other plants, but is only a fraction of its ancient size because much has been drained for farmland. The Negev Desert in the south is never completely bare and sandy as one might imagine; the hills may be bare and stony but many wadis (valleys which may have a stream in the rainy season) and hollows have stunted bushes, and a good rainy season will bring a flush of grass and flowers.

CHRIST'S THORN

The climate, land forms and human habitation through the centuries have resulted in there being several different plant communities in the region:

• scrub and shrublands called *garigue* and *maquis* respectively. The former has many soft-leaved, ground-layer plants, such as Lavender, Cistus, Senecio, Rosemary, thistles and Wild Thyme; the latter is a shrubland biome typically consisting of densely growing evergreens, such as Holm Oak, Kermes Oak, Tree Heath, Strawberry Tree, Sage, Juniper, Buckthorn, Spurge Olive and Myrtle;

• grasslands;

• woodlands of oak and pine, and forests, distinguished from woods by having a closed canopy, of mostly evergreen oaks and pines.

Many of these species can be firmly identified in the Bible, as described in the following chapters.

WILD TREES

When the Lord God made the earth and the heavens – and no shrub of the field had yet appeared on the earth and no plant of the fields had yet sprung up, for the Lord God had not sent rain on the earth, and there was no man to work the ground, but streams came up from the earth and watered the whole surface of the ground – the Lord God formed the man from the dust of the ground and breathed into his nostrils the breath of life, and the man became a living being.
Now the Lord God had planted a garden in the east, in Eden, and there he put the man he had formed. And the Lord God made all kinds of trees grow out of the ground – trees that were pleasing to the eye and good for food.

GENESIS
CH. 2, VV. 4-9

So wrote the author of this maybe 4,000 years ago; part of an explanation of the creation of the world. The creation story of the appearance in steady order of fish, plants, animals and birds in chapters 1 and 2 of Genesis does not prevent many God-fearing people today from believing in science and evolution, and understanding the explanations of climatologists, geographers, zoologists and botanists, who describe the Mediterranean basin as one of five regions in the world to have a distinct climate (see p. 6) and the effect this has on the flora.

Our examination of specific trees really begins with the wanderings of Abraham and the Israelites after Abraham was told he was to leave his homeland in Mesopotamia in the 17th century BC and go west to a new land:

The Lord had said to Abram, "Leave your country, your people and your father's household and go to the land I will show you." ... So Abram, left as

GENESIS CH. 12, vv. 1-7

the Lord had told him ... and they set out for the land of Canaan, and they arrived there. Abram travelled through the land as far as the site of the great tree of Moreh at Shechem ... The Lord appeared to Abram and said, "To your offspring I will give this land." So he built an altar there to the Lord, who had appeared to him.

A famous sanctuary already existed at Shechem, which is on the edge of the Plain of Philistia to the west of the Dead Sea. A great tree was often a special feature of such a holy place, so it was a natural place for Abram to pitch camp. A more telling reason is that clearly Abram continued to worship the one true God, and it is thought that he camped here so that his own large herds of sheep, cattle and goats did not damage the cultivated land of the Canaanites. We have then perhaps the first written reference to mankind being thoughtful about his relationship with the environment, the study of which we call *ecology*. Abram's animals could graze under the trees in the wooded foothills. This holy site is also mentioned later in the beginning of Genesis ch. 35:

OAK

> *Then God said to Jacob [Abram's grandson], "Go*
> *up to Bethel and settle there, and build an altar*
> *there to God who appeared to you when you were*
> *fleeing from your brother Esau."*

Jacob does so by the tree at Shechem, which is named as an oak in verse 4. He calls the place El Bethel, which means God of Bethel. The holiness of the site was further emphasized and the tree named when:

 GENESIS
CH. 35, V. 8

> *Deborah, Rebekah's nurse died* [Rebekah was mother of Esau and Jacob] *and was buried under the oak below Bethel. So it was named Allon Bacuth* [which means Tree of Weeping].

There is also 'a great tree' mentioned in 1 Samuel ch. 10 and Judges ch. 9. Only one of the references names the tree as an oak. The association between individual trees and people has a long history, not just in Bible times. In Europe, the Roman writer Pliny the Elder (23–79 AD) wrote that the veneration of trees was a universal custom. In North America giant Californian Redwoods *Sequoia* sp. were venerated (and still are, if the number of visitors is anything to go by). There the famous writer about the environment, Henry David Thoreau, declared in the mid 1850s (in *Atlantic Monthly*) that mankind needed forests 'for inspiration and our own true recreation'. In England the association was recorded in Thomas Hardy's novel *The Woodlanders*, (published 1887), and in the present day The Woodland Trust and The National Trust have a plan called The Ancient Tree Hunt to make a database of all its great and ancient trees; so far 113,000 have been uploaded, a very high proportion of which are oaks, and many more are waiting to be dealt with!

Abram had a rich feeling for the sacredness of land and what grows there, and it was not long before he became even more conscious of the danger of overgrazing, agreeing with his nephew Lot, who had travelled with his people and herds with Abram, that they should separate. Lot chose the plain of Jordan near Sodom, and Abram went in the opposite direction to the hills of Hebron, and settled among 'the great trees of Mamre' (Genesis ch. 13, v. 18). It is not surprising that Abram chose the land of the oaks to settle in. This was very near the holy site at Shechem. Once again he prevented what might have been environmental damage and tribal strife by keeping away from existing settlements. He almost certainly was in well-wooded oak habitat.

In Canaan, which is how modern Israel was known in Abram's time, there were several species of oak, of which the most widespread was the Kermes Oak (*Quercus coccifera*). It is native to the Mediterranean region, is an evergreen scrub oak, growing up to 5 m (16 ft) tall, but rarely taller than 2 m (6 ft), and has stiff, spiny leaves. The tree is an important food plant for a Kermes Scale insect *Porphyrophora/Kermes/Coccus* spp., one of a group of insects from which a crimson red dye is obtained from the female. The dye was known as early as the 8th century BC. As many as 20,000 insects were needed to produce about 300 gm (10 oz) of the dye. The name *Canaan* actually means 'Land of Purple' because of the importance to the economy of the dyeing industry. Today the tree's distribution is much reduced by the spread of the larger (up to 25 m/80 ft tall) Evergreen or Holm Oak (*Quercus ilex*), and by deforestation for the production of charcoal and for agricultural ground. Kermes Oak is a hardy tree, able to flourish on rough, hilly ground, saplings from its acorns grow easily, and it can withstand quite heavy grazing. Abram settled well!

Later the Lord appeared to Abraham near the great trees of Mamre and promised that Sarah, his wife, would have a son, and indeed Isaac was born. But it was not the end of the story of the oak and its relationship to God and the Israelites. Towards the end of Joshua's life, in the late 1300s BC, he assembled all the tribes of Israel together again at Shechem and there they witnessed that:

JOSHUA
CH. 24, VV. 24-26

"We will serve the Lord our God and obey him."
On that day Joshua made a covenant for the
people and there at Shechem he drew up for them
decrees and laws. And Joshua recorded these
things in the Book of the Law of God
[now preserved in the book Deuteronomy].
Then he took a large stone and set it up there
under the oak near the holy place of the Lord.

That was the seventh memorial that the Israelites had erected to remind them of what the Lord had done for them through faithful leaders such as Moses and Joshua, even though they had several times forsaken the Lord and worshipped other gods. Seven was considered the number of completeness, so this memorial under the sacred tree at Shechem was especially holy for the Israelites.

During all the time of wandering for 40 years in the desert led by Moses, and the following years in Canaan led by Joshua, the Israelites had carried the tablets of the Ten Commandments in the Ark of the Covenant.

When Moses was on Mount Sinai talking to God:

The Lord said to Moses, "Tell the Israelites to bring me an offering ... offerings of gold, silver, bronze, coloured yarn and fine linen, ram skins dyed red and hides of sea-cows, acacia wood, olive oil, spices for anointing oil and incense ... Then have them make a chest of acacia wood ... and poles of acacia wood to insert on the sides of the chest to carry it. Then put in the Ark the Testimony [i.e. The Ten Commandments] *which I will give you.* ⌇

The poles to support the tent and the surrounding walls, which together made up the travelling, portable Tabernacle [forerunner of the Temple], the table and the altar inside it, were also made of acacia. Beyond these furnishings was curtained off the Holy of Holies where the Ark of the Covenant was kept; only the High priest was allowed there.

There are hundreds of species of acacias, related to mimosas, across the world, growing in tropical or warm climates. Most of those in the Middle East are not tall trees but are hardy, thorny bushes or shrubs just a few metres tall, which are a distinctive feature of semi-desert. Almost certainly the 'burning bush' from which God spoke to Moses was an acacia. Maybe it was the one we now know as Negev Acacia (*Acacia gerrardii*) and is common on the Sinai peninsula where Moses had his meeting with God. As they wandered after they left Egypt, the commonest tree the Israelites would have seen would have been the acacia. It is a hard, enduring, close-grained wood, which is avoided by wood-eating insects, so it makes good furniture. *Acacia seyal* is thought to be the species known in Hebrew as the *shittah-tree*, which supplied the *shittim-wood* as recorded in Exodus for the building of the Ark.

Moses said that the Lord had chosen Bezalel to be chief craftsman in command of the skilled men who were to make the travelling temple, The Tabernacle and the Ark.

⌇ EXODUS
CH. 37, V. 1

Bezalel made the Ark of acacia wood – two and a half cubits long, a cubit wide, and a cubit and a half high [i.e. about 1.1 m/3¾ ft long x 0.7 m/2¼ ft wide and high].

The Ark was designed to be carried, fixed at the base to two long acacia poles. But the Ark and the supports to the Tabernacle were not the only things made of wood. The furnishings in the Holy of Holies, the table, the altar of incense and the altar of burnt offerings were also made of acacia.

Apart from the very detailed description of the building of the Ark in Exodus, acacia is mentioned only twice elsewhere, in the retelling of the Ark's construction in Deuteronomy, and in this poetic rendering by the prophet Isaiah of words of help and hope from God to the Israelites who were in exile in Babylon in the 6th century BC:

ISAIAH
CH. 41, vv. 18-20

I will turn the desert into pools of water,
and the parched ground into springs.
I will put in the desert
the cedar and the acacia, the myrtle and the olive.
I will set pines in the wasteland,
the fir and the cypress together,
so that people may see and know,
may consider and understand,
that the hand of the Lord has done this,
the Holy One of Israel has created it.

Earlier the prophet had described how the wooded landscape changed, firstly deforested by felling, then being restored naturally (ch. 14, vv. 5–8). For centuries the kings of Babylon and Assyria had sent woodsmen to fell and take away cedars, *Cedrus libani* in particular, because they were greatly prized in construction. When King Solomon wanted to build a temple, he no doubt remembered that his father King David had built a palace using cedar logs and carpenters sent by King Hiram of Tyre (2 Samuel ch. 5). Hiram remembered too:

ACACIA

1 KINGS
CH. 5, VV. 1-9

When Hiram king of Tyre heard that Solomon had been anointed king to succeed his father David, he sent envoys to Solomon ... [and Solomon replied saying] "Give orders that cedars of Lebanon be cut for me. My men will work with yours, and I will pay you for your men whatever wages you set." ... So Hiram sent word to Solomon: "I have received the message you sent me and will do all you want in providing the cedar and pine logs. My men will haul them down from Lebanon to the sea, and I will float them in rafts by sea to the place you specify."

All this began in the fourth year of Solomon's reign, c.966 BC and took about seven years to complete, involving thousands of men, mostly non-Israelite conscripts, organized by Adoniram, who had done the same responsible work for King David. The temple's measurements are carefully recorded in 1 Kings ch. 5 v. 8 and 2 Chronicles ch. 1, v. 7: 60 cubits long, 20 cubits wide and 30 high, i.e about 27 x 9 x 13.5 m (90 x 30 x 45 ft). The temple was roofed with beams and cedar planks; beams of cedar attached side rooms to the building; and the interior walls of the temple were lined from floor to ceiling with cedar boards, so that no stone could be seen. The floor was covered with pine planks, which were most probably from the Cypress (*Cupressus sempervirens*), the third most valuable tree at this time, alongside the oak and the cedar.

The Holy of Holies was built within the main building, also using much cedar wood, but having the five-sided door jambs and the doors themselves made of olive wood (*Olea europaea*) (but see also Chapter 2, p. 30). On the walls around the temple, palm trees and open flowers were carved, which made the whole place seem like a recreation of The Garden of Eden. Two large cherubims, carved from olive wood and covered with gold, embellished the inner sanctuary, and stood as guardians by the Ark.

Solomon also built a huge Palace of the Forest of Lebanon for himself (1 Kings ch. 7), with four rows of cedar columns supporting 45 cedar roof beams, and much cedar wood panelling from floor to ceiling. Although the scriptures note precisely the number of items in the temple's furnishings, we are not told how much timber was felled and used. The deforestation caused just to complete this project must have been considerable, and appears to go counter to the King's desire to decorate the interior with splendid carvings of God's creation.

Was Solomon's desire to build the best he could imagine for God's house any different from that of the godly men in Europe who built the enormous Christian cathedrals of Canterbury, Notre Dame and St Peter's? Still today mankind builds huge temples or churches, because that seems the best way he can show his devotion to God. The National Cathedral in Brasilia, Brazil, the extraordinary La Sagrada Familia cathedral in Barcelona and the Crystal Cathedral of glass in Garden Grove, California, USA, are just three spectacular, modern examples.

Time, along with the exploitation of the Cedar's wood, has led to a decrease in the number of Cedar trees in Lebanon. However, Lebanon is still known for its Cedars, as they are the emblem of the country and the symbol on the Lebanese flag. The trees survive in mountainous areas, where they are the dominant tree species. This is the case on the slopes of Mount Makmel that tower over the Kadisha valley, where the Cedars of God are found at an altitude of more than 2,000 m (6,600 ft). Four trees have reached a height of 35 m (115 ft) and their trunks are 12–14 metres (39–46 ft) in diameter.

CEDAR

In many cultures today people plant a tree as a memorial to a significant event in their lives. So it was in Abraham's life. He moved into the region of the Negev and met Abimelech, King of Gerar, on the edge of Philistine territory. The king tried to take Sarah for his wife (Abraham had said she was his sister not his wife; the story is worth reading!), but the confusion was resolved and a treaty was sworn between them:

 GENESIS
CH. 21, vv. 31-33

So that place was called Beersheba,
because the two men swore an oath there.
After the treaty had been made at Beersheba,
Abimelech and Phicol the commander of his forces
returned to the land of the Philistines. Abraham
planted a tamarisk tree in Beersheba, and there he
called upon the name of the Lord, the Eternal God.

The Tamarisk (*Tamarix aphylla*) is a small shrub or tree that can thrive in arid regions. Its rather feathery, leafy branches provide welcome shade, and its dense spikes of pink flowers make it a noticeable feature of the landscape. It was common for leaders to hold official

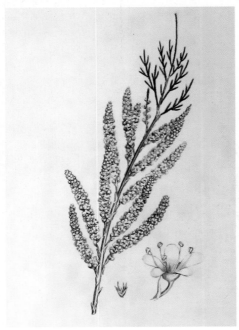

meetings under special trees. Saul had an angry meeting with his commanders under a Tamarisk tree when he learned that David, who had fled Saul's anger, had been discovered (Genesis ch. 22), and after Saul's death in battle, he was buried under a Tamarisk at Jabesh, south of the sea of Galilee (1 Samuel ch. 31).

Most Jewish holidays show a close link between events in their history and the agricultural life they lived. One such festival, 'The Festival of Booths or Tabernacles' known by them as Sukkot, is still celebrated by the faithful for seven days from the 15th day of the seventh month of Tishri (part of our September/October). It is also known as the Festival of the Ingathering; in other words

TAMARISK

it is a harvest festival, celebrating the bringing in of all the fruit and crops to storehouses. This is one of the Israelites' three Pilgrimage Festivals (with Passover or the Feast of Unleavened Bread to remember the escape from Egypt, and the Festival of Weeks or Harvest, to celebrate the first barley harvest [see also chapter 3]).

Citron

Myrtle

God said to Moses:

 LEVITICUS
CH. 23, VV. 40-43

On the first day you are to take choice fruit from the trees, and palm fronds, leafy branches and poplars [or willows], *and rejoice before the Lord your God for seven days … All native born Israelites are to live in booths so that your descendants will know that I made the Israelites live in booths when I brought them out of Egypt.*

The booth is a temporary shelter. Still today, orthodox Jews in particular will make a booth from willow and palm fronds, decorated with myrtle, and with an offering of fruit, the citron. These are samples of the four trees that God names, as described below.

The first tree God specially names is the 'choice fruit' (Leviticus ch. 23, v. 40), or as the *Authorised Version* calls it, 'the most majestic fruit'. Although not named, centuries ago scholars who wrote the commentary on the Hebrew Bible, called the Talmud, declared it was the Etrog or Citron (*Citrus medica*), a relative of the lemon, and one of the four original citrus fruits from which all types were developed. Then and now it symbolizes in the festival hope for fertility and an abundant harvest.

A second tree, the Date Palm (*Phoenix dactylifera*) probably originated in the Middle East, but it is now so widely cultivated that its original wild state is unknown. It soon became very important in the life of the Israelites as they wandered the desert because palms need water, so where they grow indicates an oasis, a safe place to camp. The people soon learned that they not only provide fronds to shelter under and for building, but also high energy food (see chapter 2), camel fodder and fibres for weaving baskets and rope.

When the Israelites came to the banks of the River Jordan they found the most abundant plant there was the willow, sometimes translated into English as the poplar (*Salix* sp.). The tree is so dependant on a good supply of water that it became a symbol of the Jews' prayer beseeching God to save them from drought by bringing the winter rains, which would enable them to prepare the land for next year's crops.

The fourth tree which the Jews traditionally brought to the booths was one the children of Israel found when they reached the Promised Land and discovered the hills were covered with forest, much of it dense thickets of Myrtle (*Myrtus communis*). Unlike the willow, this tree does not need much water, and sprigs of it will remain fresh for weeks. It is an aromatic plant and may grow more than 5 m (about 16½ feet) high. The opposite leaves are thick and

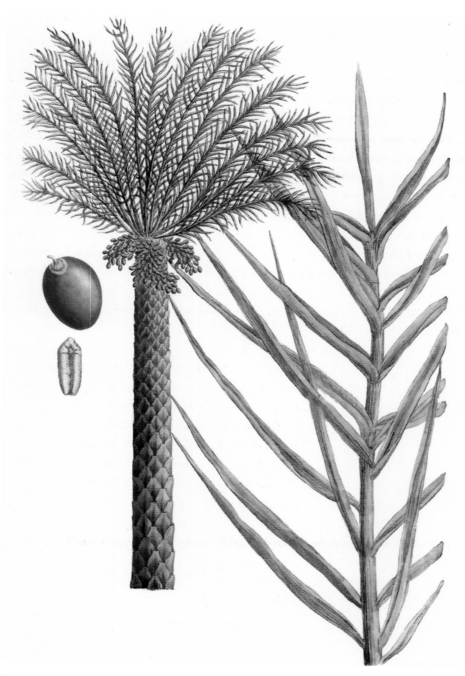

Date Palm

lustrous, with many small, translucent, oil-bearing glands. The solitary white flowers, about 1.8 cm (¾ inch) long, are borne on short stalks. The fruit is a purplish black, many-seeded berry. Myrtol, a volatile oil found in most parts of the plant, was formerly used as an antiseptic and tonic. In ancient times the Myrtle was a symbol of immortality, and so, by extension, a symbol of prosperity and success. The original settlers in the Promised Land clearly felt God was giving them a reminder of this and the hope for a successful harvest.

Perhaps the most well-known tree in the New Testament is the one commonly referred to as the Sycamore, but it is not the woodland or hedgerow tree familiar to many people in Britain. It is more properly translated as the Sycamore-fig (*Ficus sycomorus*). In St Luke's gospel we read the story of Zacchaeus, the tax collector who climbed such a tree (see p. 38). The tree produces good fruit and had been cultivated since at least the third millenium BC. The ancient Egyptians called it The Tree of Life. The Jews grew it too, but it would appear that one or several were growing wild by the road in Jericho. It can grow as tall as 20 m (65 ft), has a wide canopy and was certainly sturdy enough for a grown man to climb high into it. (See also Chapter 2 for details of its fruit.)

In 1825 the American poet William Cullen Bryant published *Forest Hymn*, in which he declared that:

> *The groves were God's first temples. Ere man learned*
> *To hew the shaft and lay the architrave*
> *And spread the roof above them – ere he framed*
> *The lofty vault, to gather and roll back*
> *The sound of anthems; in the darkling wood*
> *Amidst its cool and silence, he knelt down,*
> *And offered to the Mightiest solemn thanks*
> *And supplication.*

Thus it was in the time of the Patriarchs, and for many believers, so it is still.

SYCOMORE-FIG

CHAPTER 11

FRUITS AND VEGETABLES

Today when someone receives an unexpected gift, which fulfils a need – such as some money or a prize – the cry goes up, 'Manna from heaven!' Many will understand what is meant, but many may not really know what manna is. The answer is about 3,500 years old. The Israelites have been captives in Egypt for many years and at last have been freed by Pharaoh, have miraculously crossed the Red Sea, which then drowned the pursuing Egyptian charioteers, and been led by Moses into the desert:

In the desert the whole community grumbled against Moses and Aaron. The Israelites said to them, "If only we had died by the Lord's hand in Egypt. There we sat around pots of meat and ate all the food we wanted, but you have brought us out into this desert to starve this entire assembly to death."
Then the Lord said to Moses, "I will rain down bread from heaven for you. The people are to go out each day and gather enough for that day."

Moses and Aaron told the people this good news and the later promise of God that "at twilight you will eat meat, and in the morning you will be filled with bread."

⮑ EXODUS
CH. 16, VV. 2-4
AND 13-15

That evening Quail came and covered the camp, and in the morning there was a layer of dew around the camp. When the dew was gone, thin flakes like frost on the ground appeared on the desert floor. When the Israelites saw it they said to each other, "What is it?" For they did not know what it was. Moses said to them, "It is the bread the Lord has given you to eat." ⮑

Almond

Clearly this was not bread as we know it, but it is one of the first times we read in the Bible about a named food. As a miraculous example of God's bounty, it is a fitting start to our thinking about what the Israelites ate in the way of fruits, cereals and vegetables. Our word 'manna' comes from the Hebrew words that the Israelites spoke in their grumbling to Moses: 'man hu' which simply means 'what is it?'.

Our understanding of what it might be has changed over the years. A traditional explanation was that it was a sweet secretion from the Tamarisk Tree. More recent study has discovered that this 'manna' is produced by scale insects, which feed on the Tamarisks. The insects consume huge amounts of sap to obtain carbohydrates, and excrete the excess as 'honeydew'. The white, frosty looking residue was:

 NUMBERS
CH. 11, VV. 7-8

like coriander seed, white, and the taste of it was like wafers made with honey, and the people ground it in mills or beat it in mortars, then boiled it in pots and made cakes of it; and the taste of it was like the taste of cakes baked with oil.

A huge amount of this would have been needed to feed the Israelites, which to many readers has seemed ridiculous. We must remember, however, that a perfectly natural explanation misses the point that the manna and quails in the desert were a miraculous gift from God. That wonderful providence is recalled by Jesus when He called Himself the bread of life. He says to the disciples:

 ST JOHN
CH. 6, VV. 49-51

Your forefathers ate the manna in the desert, yet they died. But here is the bread which comes down from heaven, which a man may eat and not die. I am the living bread that came down from heaven. If anyone eats of this bread, he will live for ever.

Long before the exodus from Egypt and the miraculous manna, is the story of the Jews' arrival there. There was famine in Palestine and Joseph's brothers are sent to Egypt by their father, Jacob, to buy grain. They meet Joseph but do not recognise him. He says he will help if the youngest brother is brought to him. So a second journey is made. Jacob says:

GENESIS
CH. 43, V. 11

If it must be then do this: Put some of the best products of the land in your bags and take them down to the man as a gift – a little balm, and a little honey, some spices and myrrh, some pistachio nuts and almonds.

Carvings of Almond flowers were on the woodwork of the tabernacle, which held the Ark of the Covenant. The beauty of Almond flowers (or maybe Walnut) is probably the species mentioned in *Song of Songs* and in Jeremiah's prophecy. The Almond tree is revealed to be even more important in the story of the Israelites' anger with Moses and Aaron, and the revolution stirred up by Korah of the tribe of Levi against Moses and Aaron. Moses says God will sort the problem out, and so:

NUMBERS
CH. 17, VV. 1-5 & 8

The Lord said to Moses, "Speak to the Israelites and get twelve staffs from them, one for each of the ancestral tribes. Write the name of each man on his staff. On the staff of Levi write Aaron's name, for there must be one staff for the head of each ancestral tribe. Place them in the Tent of the Meeting in front of the Testimony, where I meet with you. The staff belonging to the man I choose will sprout, and I will rid myself of this constant grumbling against you by the Israelites.
... The next day Moses entered the Tent of the Testimony and saw that Aaron's staff, which represented the house of Levi, had not only sprouted but had budded, blossomed and produced almonds.

So there was now no uncertainty. The importance of the role of Aaron the priest and his sons in the worship of Israel was firmly grounded, and symbolically shown by the placing of Aaron's staff near the Ark of the Covenant.

Clearly it is a fruit tree that has played a sacred part in Jewish life. The Almond (*Prunus dulcis*) is native to the Middle East and South Asia. It grows up to 10 m (33 ft) tall and bears fruit in the third year. It is thought that the tree was first cultivated in ancient times in the

POMEGRANATE

Levant, so Jacob would have been familiar with groves of the trees.

Soon after the Almond trees blossomed, the scarlet blooms of the Pomegranate (*Punica granatum*) appeared. It has been cultivated since ancient times from Egypt to Mesopotamia. When Moses talked to God and received the Ten Commandments, he was given a detailed description of the design of the priest's robes that Aaron had to wear when he entered the Holy Place:

 EXODUS
CH. 28, V. 31-35

Make the robe of the ephod* entirely of blue cloth, with an opening for the head in the centre. There shall be a woven edge like a collar round this opening, so that it will not tear. Make pomegranates of blue, purple and scarlet yarn round the hem of the robe, with gold bells between them. The gold bells and the pomegranates are to alternate round the hem of the robe. Aaron must wear it when he ministers.

* An ephod was a sleeveless vestment worn by the High Priest.

The ripe fruit contains hundreds of tasty seeds. In the Middle East it had long been considered to be a fertility symbol, and its sacred significance became part of the Israelites' beliefs when they made Aaron's robes.

Later, scouts sent by Moses to see what the Promised Land looked like, came back with various fruits:

NUMBERS
CH. 13, V. 23

they cut off a branch bearing a single cluster of grapes. Two of them carried it on a pole between them, along with some pomegranates and figs.

Clearly the size of the grape cluster and the variety of fruits were indications of the goodness of the land into which God was leading them. Further more, pomegranates were listed by God when he said to Moses:

 DEUTERONOMY
CH. 8, VV. 6-9

Observe the commands of the Lord your God,
walking in His ways, and revering him. For the
Lord your God is bringing you into a good land –
a land with streams and pools of water, …
a land with wheat and barley, vines and fig trees,
pomegranates, olive oil and honey; a land where
bread will not be scarce and you will lack nothing.

King Sennacherib, who besieged Jerusalem in 701 BC, also made use of a similar description for Israel when promising the inhabitants of Jerusalem that he would exile them to a country of like fertility:

 2 KINGS
CH. 18, V. 32

Make peace with me and come out with me.
Then every one of you will eat from his own vine
and fig tree and drink water from his own cistern,
until I come and take you to a land like your own,
a land of grain and new wine, a land of bread
and vineyards, a land of olive trees and
honey. Choose life not death!

The Israelites did not leave, but Isaiah, the prophet, told their king, Hezekiah, that eventually, because of their sins, they would be exiled to Babylon – and that did happen, in 586 BC.

The list is known as the Seven Species, the *Shiv'at Ha-Minim*, being the special products of the land of Israel. Pictures of the fruit appeared on ancient Judaean coins, and decorative silver globes shaped like pomegranates sometimes cover the handles of scrolls of the Torah.

The olive oil mentioned in the quotation from Deuteronomy indicates that the Israelites cooked with this oil. The wild Olive (*Olea europaea*) grows in the groves of Upper Galilee and Carmel. It is a prickly shrub producing small fruits. Olive trees have always been the most extensively distributed and the most conspicuous in the landscape of the Mediterranean region. Production of olive oil has been traced as far back as 2400 BC in clay documents found near Aleppo in Syria. Today, Israel produces only about half of the oil it needs each year, so imports are vital because the olive is numbered among the seven foods with which Israel is blessed.

Olive

There are many varieties of cultivated olives, some whose fruit is suitable for oil, and some for food as preserved olives. Its foliage is dense and when it becomes old, the fairly tall trunk acquires a unique pattern of twists and protuberances on its bark. There are trees in Israel estimated to be 1,000 years old, such as the one in the garden of Gethsemane in Jerusalem. In old age the tree becomes hollow but the trunk continues to grow thicker, at times achieving a circumference of 6 m (20 ft). The olive tree blossoms at the beginning of summer and its fruit ripens about the time of the early rains in October. The fruit is first green, but later becomes black.

The bounty of Israel is frequently described as 'corn, wine, and oil' (Deuteronomy ch. 7, v. 13, et al.), that is, grain, vines and olives, which formed the basis of Israel's economy. When the Israelites conquered the land they found extensive olive plantations (Deuteronomy ch. 6, v. 11). Western Galilee, the territory of Asher (who was Jacob's son), was – and is – especially rich in olives, so much so that Asher will 'bathe his feet in oil' (ch. 33, v. 24). Olive trees flourish in mountainous areas too, even among the rocks, thus producing 'oil out of the flinty rock' (Deuteronomy ch. 32, v. 13). Outside the walls of Jerusalem is The Mount of Olives (Zecharaiah ch. 14, v. 4). It is named in Hebrew, *Har ha-Mishḥah*, 'the mount of oil'. The fruit of the olive also develops well in the plain between Mt Hermon and the coast (the Shephelah Lowland), where it grows near sycamores. These crops were so precious that David appointed special overseers to manage the plantations. So far as we know David did not raise taxes; he financed his court by wealth from his extensive land holdings, commerce, plunder and tribute from subjugated kingdoms – so the first two of these depended on his orchards being well looked after:

1 CHRONICLES
CH. 27, V. 28

Baal-Hanan the Gederite was in charge of the olive and sycamore trees in the western foothills. Joash was in charge of the supplies of olive oil.

We don't often think of there being parables in the Old Testament, compared with the many that Jesus told. But there is an important one in the book of Judges. After Gideon's death in 1122 BC, Abimelech by sweet talk and violence became leader. The people were spoken to by the prophet Jotham. He told them a parable about the day when the trees went out to appoint a king for themselves. The olive was the first to be chosen by the trees. But it refused. So did the fig-tree and the vine. Lastly the thornbush foretold dire consequences if Abimelech had become king by dishonourable means and no-one came to rest in its shade (Judges ch. 9, vv. 8–15). The bush was a fitting symbol for Abimelech. The curse of Jotham did fall on the people who had chosen him (Judges ch. 9, v. 57).

The olive tree is full of beauty, especially when laden with fruit, as the prophet tells us: 'a leafy olive-tree, fair with goodly fruit' (Jeremiah ch. 11, v. 6). It is an evergreen, and the righteous who take refuge in the protection of God are compared to it:

> PSALM *But I am like an olive tree*
> 52, v. 10 *flourishing in the house of God.*

As we have read, the olive is long-lived, sometimes growing into a marvellous, twisted, gnarled tree. The 'olive shoots' of Psalm 128, v. 3 are actually the saplings that sprout from its roots and protect the trunk and, if it is cut down, they ensure its continued existence. This is the simile referred to in the words:

> PSALM *"Your wife will be like a fruitful vine within your house;*
> 128, v. 3 *your sons will be like olive saplings round about your table."*

The psalmist chose a precious plant which helped to keep the people alive, to describe as best he could the blessings and prosperity of having a family.

Olive wood is very hard and beautifully grained, making it suitable for the manufacture of small articles and ornaments; the hollow trunk of the adult tree, however, renders it unsuitable for pieces of furniture. Some commentators therefore say that the olive cannot be the wood (*ez. shemen*) from which the doors of Solomon's Temple were made:

> 1 KINGS *For the entrance of the inner sanctuary he made*
> CH. 6, v. 31 *doors of olive wood with five-sided jambs.*

The entrance to the main hall had similar doors from olive wood, so the scripture says.

After the fruit is formed, the tree may be attacked by the olive fly, causing the fruit to rot and fall off (Deuteronomy ch. 28, v. 40). The fruits are arranged on the thin branches in parallel rows like ears of corn (Zecharaiah ch. 4, v. 12). After ripening, the fruit is harvested in two different ways, by beating the branches with sticks or by hand picking. The former is quicker but many branches are broken and this diminishes successive harvests. This method was used in biblical times, the Bible commanding that the fruits on the fallen branches are to be a gift to the poor:

 DEUTERONOMY
CH. 24, V. 20

When you beat the olives from your trees,
do not go over the branches a second time.
Leave what remains for the alien [immigrants],
the fatherless and the widow.

The second method was the more usual from about 200 AD onwards according to the early part of the Talmud, the commentary on the Hebrew scriptures. It was termed *masik* ('harvesting olives'), the fingers being drawn down the branches in a milking motion so that the olives fall into the hand. By this method the harvested olives remained whole, whereas the beaten olives were often bruised.

There were olives of different varieties and different sizes, to be processed into oil for cooking and in lamps, to be preserved (the best species being *kelofsin* or *keloska* olives) and for use in religious rituals, for healing, strength and consecration. Perhaps the best-known example in the Old Testament of the last is when Samuel, after the death of King Saul, is led by God to anoint the youngest son of Jesse:

 SAMUEL
CH. 16, V. 16

So Samuel took the horn of oil and anointed him
in the presence of his brothers, and from that day
on the Spirit of the Lord came upon David in power.

In the New Testament, the story of an unnamed woman at the home of Simon the Pharisee is particularly well known. Jesus says to Simon:

 ST LUKE
CH. 7, VV. 44-46

I came into your house. You did not give me any
water for my feet [which in these times was the minimal gesture of hospitality to show to a visitor who had walked a dusty road in sandals].
You did not put oil on my head, but she has
poured perfume on my feet.

The oil's everyday use in the kitchen is told in the story from the ninth century BC, of Elisha the prophet and the widow's jar of oil. Her husband has died and his creditor is coming to take her two boys away. She cries out to Elisha for help, and he replies:

*"How can I help you? Tell me,
what do you have in your house?"
"Your servant has nothing at all,"
she said, "except a little oil."*

He tells her to collect as many jars as she can and pour her little bit of oil into all the jars she collects. She fills every one!

∽ 2 KINGS
CH. 4, vv. 1-7

*She went and told the man of God and he said,
"Go, sell the oil and pay your debts.
You and your sons can live on what is left."* ∾

The importance and power of olive oil is wonderfully told in that story.

Finally, the modern symbol of peace, an olive leaf in the beak of a dove, can trace its origin back to the story of Noah's dove, which returned to the Ark carrying an olive leaf (Genesis ch. 8, v. 11).

To those who live in the Middle East, the Palm Tree, that is the Date Palm (*Phoenix dactylifera*), is probably as important or more important than the olive. One of the oldest cultivated fruit crops, the Date Palm has long been harvested for its tasty, fleshy fruit, which is a staple food for many people across North Africa and Arabia. There are many hundreds of varieties of this species, each of which is grown for commercial purposes, making the Date Palm perhaps the second most familiar palm species after the Coconut Palm (*Cocos nucifera*). It grows with an imposing, tall, slender, straight trunk, which has a spiralling pattern on the bark, with

DATE PALM

long, feather-like leaves, which are greenish-grey in colour and have spines on the lower third of the stem. On the upper part of the crown, the leaves stand pointing upwards, but on the lower part, the leaves curve towards the ground. The leaves are rigid, long and pointed, with as many as 200 leaflets growing on each side of the stem. The flowers are clustered into elongated, sheathed inflorescences borne on separate male and female plants; the male's are white and fragrant, and the female's smaller, and more yellowish or cream in colour. The sugar-rich fruit, which is commonly known as a date, is a large, oblong berry that is dark orange when ripe, and may grow up to 7.5 cm (3 in) in length on some cultivated varieties.

2 Chonicles 28, v.15 records that Jericho is 'the city of palm trees'. Ezekiel chh. 40 & 41 record his vision of a new temple and how a great deal of the structure and carving was with palm wood. But there are only two references to palms in the New Testament. St John, the Gospel writer in his later great vision:

 REVELATION
CH. 7, V. 9

looked and there before me was a great multitude that no-one could count, from every nation, tribe, people and language, standing before the throne and in front of the Lamb. They were wearing white robes and were holding palm branches in their hands.

Since ancient times palm branches have been used on festive occasions but to Christians throughout the world the most memorable reference to palms is at the beginning of the Easter story:

 ST JOHN
CH. 12, VV. 12-14

The next day the great crowd that had come for the Feast [of the Passover] heard that Jesus was on his way to Jerusalem. They took palm branches and went out to meet him, shouting,
"Blessed is he who comes in the name of the Lord!"
"Hosanna!"
"Blessed is the King of Israel!"

All four Gospel writers tell of Jesus' triumphant entry into Jerusalem on what Christians call Palm Sunday, the week before the next Sunday which is Easter Day. But only St John names *palm* branches.

Fig trees are recorded in both the Old and New Testaments. To cover their nakedness and shame in the Garden of Eden, Adam and Eve sewed fig leaves together; King Sennacherib promised each Israelite could have his own fig tree; King David appointed Baal-Hanan, the Gederite, as overseer of his sycamores; Jesus told a parable about a fig tree, and Zacchaeus climbed one. They were all referring to fruit from the same family but from two different trees: the Common Fig (*Ficus carica*) and the Sycomore-fig (*Ficus sycomorus*). Sadly, by association, most references today incorrectly refer to a Sycomore-fig, because the English translators cannot get out of their minds the name of the common English tree, the Sycomore (*Acer pseudoplatanus*), which is related to maples not figs. The fig tree is the first to be named with a common name in the Bible, and the third of all trees to be mentioned after the Tree of Life and the Tree of the Knowledge of Good and Evil (Genesis ch. 3, v. 7).

Common Figs were (and are) cultivated throughout Palestine. A summer tree in full leaf gives cool, welcome shade. Failure of their harvest would cause great distress, whether by natural or warlike means:

COMMON FIG

JEREMIAH
CH. 5, VV. 15-17

"O house of Israel," declares the Lord,
"I am bringing a distant nation against you –
an ancient and enduring nation ...
They will devour your harvests and food,
devour your sons and daughters;
they will devour your flocks and herds,
devour your vines and fig-trees."

According to the colour and quality of the fruit, farmers have distinguished several varieties. Self-sown trees are usually barren. The trees lose their leaves in winter and by the end of March are in bud again. Tiny figs form at the same time as the leaves appear, grow to about the size of a cherry, then the majority of them are blown by the wind to the ground. These 'green', 'untimely' or 'winter' figs are collected and can be eaten. Some do develop and become 'very good figs, like those that ripen early' (Jeremiah ch. 24, v. 2). They are known by Micah as 'the early figs that I crave' (Micah ch. 7, v. 1). As these are ripening, little buds of the next crop form further up the branches, to be harvested in August.

Besides being eaten fresh or dried, they are also pressed into a solid cake (1 Chronicles ch. 12, v. 40), as was prepared by Abigail for David (1 Samuel ch. 25, v. 18); or even used medicinally:

> **2 KINGS**
> CH. 20, VV. 1 & 7
>
> *In those days [late 600s BC] Hezekiah became ill and was at the point of death ... Then Isaiah said, "Prepare a poultice of figs." They did so and applied it to the boil, and he recovered.*

The other fig, the Sycomore-fig, is recorded several times, firstly when David appointed Baal-Hanaan, and later when Solomon made 'cedar as plentiful as Sycomore-fig trees in the foothills' (1 Kings ch. 10, v. 27). It is a large tree growing up to 20 m (65 ft) tall, with a dense crown of spreading branches. It is mostly found in Africa south of the Sahara, but long ago was naturalized in Egypt and Israel and grown as an orchard fruit tree. Evidence of the cultivation of Sycomore-figs in Old Testament times is told by the prophet Amos when he describes his occupation to Amaziah the priest:

> **AMOS**
> CH. 7, V. 14
>
> *I was neither a prophet nor a prophet's son, but I was a shepherd, and I also took care of Sycomore-fig trees.*

To get the tree to bear good, ripe fruit is difficult. It depends on a complex association with insects and other creatures, and the gardener having to split the top of each fig. The obscure Hebrew word to describe Amos' work is variously translated as 'dresser of', 'tend' or 'took care of', and physical evidence of the work has been found in the tombs of Ancient Egypt where the fruit was cultivated extensively from the start of the third millennium BC.

One of the most well-known stores in the Bible is found only in St Luke's gospel:

> **ST LUKE**
> CH. 19, VV. 1-4
>
> *Jesus entered Jericho and was passing through. A man was there by the name of Zacchaeus; he was a chief tax collector and was wealthy. He wanted to see who Jesus was, but being a short man he could not, because of the crowd. So he ran ahead and climbed a Sycomore-fig Tree to see him, since Jesus was coming that way.*

He did see Jesus, but more to the point Jesus saw him. St Luke writes that although Jesus was originally just passing through Jericho, He makes a point of speaking to Zacchaeus, and inviting Himself to stay at his house! Zacchaeus was thrilled, although the crowd was not: 'He's gone to be the guest of a "sinner"'. Such men in the employ of the Romans and extorting money from the Israelites were all condemned as far as the faithful were concerned. But Jesus recognized a wonderful opportunity to preach one of His most important messages. Zacchaeus repented of his greed and promised to repay what he had gained by cheating:

⁓ ST LUKE
CH. 19, vv. 9-10

Jesus said to him, "Today salvation has come to this house, because this man, too, is a son of Abraham. For the Son of man came to seek and to save what was lost." ⁓

Jesus saw that Zacchaeus was a true Jew, even though the crowd did not. It is worth emphasizing that the tree was a *Sycomore-fig*, not a *Sycamore*, which many people in Britain know as a wild tree, and was the word used in the *Authorized Version* of the Bible. Modern scholarship has corrected later translations. Also only in St Luke, Jesus tells this parable:

⁓ ST LUKE
CH. 13, vv. 6-9

A man had a fig-tree, planted in his vineyard, and he went to look for fruit on it, but did not find any. So he said to the man who took care of the vineyard, "For three years now I've been coming to look for fruit on this fig-tree and haven't found any. Cut it down! Why should it use up soil?" "Sir," the man replied, "leave it alone for one more year, and I'll dig around it and fertilise it. If it bears fruit next year, fine!, If not, then cut it down." ⁓

Jesus may have been hoping the crowd would realise that He was really referring to the Jewish nation which needed to change its ways and be more attentive to God's word, which would feed their minds and souls and make them more faithful, more 'fruitful'. We as individuals today could (or should) be mindful that the message is for us too.

In the Parable of the Prodigal Son, Jesus mentions another fruit. The son has selfishly taken his inheritance, left home for a foreign land and squandered all his money:

After he had spent everything there was a severe famine in the whole country, and he began to be in need. So he went and hired himself out to a citizen of that country, who sent him to his fields to feed pigs. He longed to fill his stomach with the pods that the pigs were eating, but no-one gave him anything.

ST LUKE
CH. 15, vv. 14-16

The point is made especially sharp by the fact that the boy has to live with pigs, which to Jews are unclean, indicating that the boy was a particularly bad sinner.

The pods were almost certainly the fruits of the Carob Tree (*Ceratonia siliqua*). It is also known as The Locust Bean and St John's Bread. These traditional names may mean that John the Baptist did not eat honey and locusts in the wilderness, but ate honey and locust-beans. It is a native of the Middle East and has been cultivated since ancient times. The use of the

Carob during a famine is probably a result of the tree's resilience to the harsh climate and drought. During a famine, the swine were given Carob pods so that they would not be a burden on the farmer's limited resources. As many will well know there is a happy ending. The son is welcomed home by his father, and is forgiven. Once again Jesus preaches a powerful message about love and the fact that God loves a sinner who repents. Today the pod is still important commercially; it is used as a thickening agent in the food industry, in the production of biscuits and cakes and as a chocolate substitute.

There is only one reference to the Pistachio (*Pistacia vera*) in the Bible: the command of Jacob to pack Pistachio nuts as part of his sons' gift

CAROB TREE

to Joseph, their brother, whom they were visiting a second time in Egypt (Genesis ch. 43, v. 11). The tree is native to the Middle East, including Israel, and has been cultivated for many centuries. The Hanging Gardens of Babylon (8th century BC) are said to have contained such trees, and at an archaeological dig in the Hula Valley, in Israel, seeds and nut-cracking tools were found and dated to 78,000 years ago!

From the first book in the Bible to the last, vineyards are mentioned. Noah, a farmer, was the first person recorded to plant a vineyard after he and his family and the animals came on land again after the flood (Genesis ch. 9, vv. 20–23). He also became the first person to drink too much and become drunk, much to the distress of his sons, Ham, Shem and Japheth. A later writer emphasized wine's power when he wrote 'Don't let wine tempt you, even though it is rich red' (Proverbs ch. 23, v. 21). Another Old Testament book has an erotic image spoken by a male lover to his beloved, which names the fruit and its temptation:

How beautiful you are and how pleasing,
O love, with your delights!
Your stature is like that of the palm,
and your breasts like clusters of fruit.
I said, "I will climb the palm tree;
I will take hold of its fruit."
May your breasts be like clusters of the vine,
the fragrance of your breath like apples,
and your mouth like the best wine. ≈

SONG OF SONGS
CH. 7, VV. 6-9

PISTACHIO

St John, writing in Revelation, the last book, sees a vision of the final judgement of the people of the world. One angel gathers all the righteous people, and another is told to harvest the rest:

REVELATION
CH. 14, VV. 18-20

"Take your sharp sickle and gather the clusters
of grapes from the earth's vine, because the grapes
are ripe." The angel swung his sickle on the earth,
gathered its grapes and threw them into the great
winepress of God's wrath. They were trampled in
the winepress outside the city, and blood flowed
out of the press ... ≈

Whatever our understanding of this apocalyptic description of the end of the world, it does tell us how the farmers of that time extracted the juice of the grapes. The winepress was a rock-hewn trough about 2.5 m (8 ft) square with a channel on one side leading to a smaller trough. Grapes were thrown in the upper trough and trampled with bare feet; the juice flowed into the lower trough, to be collected and turned into wine.

GRAPES

The Old Testament has dozens of references to grapes, vineyards and wine, which show how important it was to those people at that time. However, wine was not just for drinking, it was to be part of the regular sacrificial offerings, as recorded in Exodus ch. 29, Leviticus chh. 1–7 and Numbers ch. 28. But above all it is the Psalmist who sums up the Jews' feelings about the vine, the grape and the wine:

WINEPRESS

⤳ PSALM
104, vv. 14-15

[God] makes grass grow for the cattle,
and plants for man to cultivate –
bringing forth food from the earth:
wine that gladdens the heart of man,
oil to make his face shine,
and bread that sustains his heart. ⤳

To the Jews, the vineyard and what grew there was more than just a source of sweet food to gladden their hearts. The prophet Isaiah (749–681 BC) put it like this in a section of his prophecy often titled as *The Song of the Vineyard:*

⤳ ISAIAH
CH. 5, vv. 1-2 & 7

I will sing for the one I love
a song about his vineyard:
My loved one had a vineyard
on a fertile hillside.
He dug it up and cleared it of stones
and planted it with the choicest vines.
He built a watchtower in it
and cut out a winepress as well.
Then he looked for a crop of good grapes
but it yielded only bad fruit ...
The vineyard of the Lord Almighty
is the house of Israel,
and the men of Judah
are the garden of his delight.
And he looked for justice, but saw bloodshed;
for righteousness, but heard cries of distress. ⤳

Isaiah describes a special vineyard, then interprets it with a powerful play on words in the last two lines – in Hebrew the words for 'justice' and 'bloodshed' sound alike, as do 'righteousness' and 'distress'. There follows Isaiah's declaration of God's judgement which will come on the sinful nation of Judah, including the fact that 'a ten-acre vineyard will produce only a bath of wine' (i.e. about 36 l (8 gallons), ch. 5, v. 10), which is a very small fraction of what the harvest should be. The total depends on the quality of the grapes, the quality of the land, the density of the planting and careful husbandry; then good wine can be produced from 4–8 tons of grapes *per acre*, and that can give c. 700 l (150–160 gallons) of wine *per ton per acre*. God's punishment is a really harsh one. Jews today may believe that God's vineyard of Israel is the conquering one now, not the conquered nation Isaiah was describing, but it is certainly not peaceful.

Jesus was also adept at creating telling images from everyday life. One of His most memorable is His Parable of the Tenants of a Vineyard, which is found in Matthew, Mark and Luke, is probably based on The Song of the Vineyard, and is very likely in the mind of John when he recorded Jesus' declaration that:

 ST JOHN
CH. 15, v. 1

"I am the true vine, and my Father is the gardener."

St Matthew tells the parable in detail:

 ST MATTHEW
CH. 21, vv. 33-34

There was a landowner who planted a vineyard.
He put a wall around it, dug a winepress in it and
built a watchtower. Then he rented the vineyard
to some farmers and went away on a journey.
When the harvest time approached he sent his
servants to the tenants to collect his fruit.

But the tenants were greedy and thought they could make the vineyard their own. They killed a servant, beat and stoned others, and then the owner sent his son, who surely would be respected:

 ST MATTHEW
CH. 21, vv. 38-39

But when the tenants saw the son, they said to each
other, "This is the heir. Come let's kill him, and
take his inheritance." So they took him and threw
him out of the vineyard and killed him.

This parable was told by Jesus in Jerusalem a little while after He had angrily overturned the tables of the money-changers in the temple. It is one of his statements at this time warning the disciples of His imminent death.

St John sums up much of what Christians believe, when he records these words of Jesus:

 ST JOHN
CH. 15, vv. 1-4 & 16

I am the true vine, and my Father is the gardener. He cuts off every branch in me that bears no fruit, while every branch that does bear fruit he prunes so that it will be even more fruitful. You are already clean [i.e. pruned] *because of the word I have spoken to you. Remain in me, and I will remain in you. No branch can bear fruit by itself; it must remain in the vine. Neither can you bear fruit unless you remain in me … I chose you and appointed you to go and bear fruit – fruit that will last.*

The disciples and people today still puzzle over what is meant by 'fruit'. Some think it just means that you have persuaded someone to be a Christian. I think it is to be more widely understood as described by St Paul:

GALATIANS
CH. 5, vv. 16, 22-23

So I say, live by the Spirit, and you will not gratify the desires of sinful nature. But the fruit of the Spirit is love, joy, peace, patience, kindness, goodness, faithfulness, gentleness and self-control. Against such things there is no law.

That is a rich harvest of fruit indeed, nine grapes in one cluster, giving wine of the best quality! That is the harvest which will enrich the Christians' lives and the church's evangelism, and ensure all believers do love their neighbours as themselves.

CHAPTER III

OTHER CROPS

The beginning of the story of the Jews is either lost in myth and legend or, depending on your point of view, recorded carefully in the first book of the Bible, Genesis. The first word in the Hebrew text is *hereshith* ('in [the] beginning'). This is the Hebrew title of the book (our name comes from the Greek Septuagint translation), so it tells of the early history of the Hebrew world. After the stories of the Creation and the Garden of Eden we come to a family tale: the birth of two sons – Cain and Abel – to Adam and Eve.

Eventually each son brings an offering to the Lord of what they have produced. Cain brought 'some fruits' but Abel brought 'fat portions from some of the first born of his flock'. God looked favourably on Abel's generous offering but not so on Cain's casual gift. Cain was jealous that his brother was praised by God, and killed him. When God asked where his brother was, Cain gave a reply that has entered the English language as a saying from someone who claims to have nothing to do with the welfare of a sibling or acquaintance: "Am I my brother's keeper?" (v. 9). Sadly, this callous indifference to others is still widespread in the world today, and results in individuals and nations being like Cain – outcasts.

Archaeology has revealed that the early history of the people of the region did indeed keep flocks and grow crops. Abraham, Isaac and Jacob were such people; pastoral farmers, semi-nomadic, wandering to find food for their animals. On the other hand, the people of Egypt, thanks to the fertile soil along the Nile valley, were famous for their crops of grain. By Christ's time when the Romans ruled the world, Egypt was 'the bread basket' of the known world. Over the course of centuries growing crops became increasingly important, and constantly in the Old Testament the listing together of grain, wine, oil and pulses shows that these products were the principal harvests of the Palestinian farmer, and the Jews' social and religious year revolved around the several harvest periods (see p. 18).

In 1908 archaeologists digging at the ancient city of Gezer west of Jerusalem found an inscribed limestone tablet, which has become known as the Gezer Calendar:

BARLEY

two months gathering [olives] (September, October)
two months planting (November, December)
two months late sowing (January, February)
one month cutting flax (March)
one month reaping barley (April)
one month reaping and measuring grain (May)
two months pruning [vines] (June, July)
one month summer fruit (August)

Whether these are the words of a popular song or a schoolboy's memory exercise does not hide the fact that it is clear that the Palestinian farmer was toiling throughout the year. Besides the tasks listed he also had to clear the stony land ready to plough, then had to irrigate the land during the dry season, as is recorded in The *Apochrypha* (Ecclesiasticus ch. 24, vv. 30–31).

The descendants of Cain grew barley and wheat. The first reference to barley is in the recording of the dreadful catastrophes which overtook Egypt because Pharaoh refused to let the Israelites leave the country. God told Moses to tell Pharaoh:

⬿ EXODUS
CH. 9, VV. 18 & 31-32

"... at this time tomorrow I will send the worst hailstorm that has ever fallen on Egypt, from the day it was founded till now."
(The flax and barley were destroyed, since the barley was in the ear and the flax was in bloom. The wheat and spelt however, [see pp. 53–54] were not destroyed, because they ripen later.) ⬾

We will consider the two cereal grains in the order they are mentioned, which is not the same as their importance or value, as will be seen. Barley (*Hordeum vulgare*) is a cereal grain, a self-pollinating member of the grass family. Its wild ancestor grew abundantly in the Fertile Crescent of western Asia, a horseshoe shape of land from Mesopotamia to Upper Egypt. This is the very land of Cain and the Patriarchs of old, so it is perfectly natural that we should find that one of God's laws for them says:

LEVITICUS

CH. 27, V. 16

If a man dedicates to the Lord part of his family land, its value is to be set according to the amount of seed required for it – fifty shekels of silver to a homer [6 bushels or about 220 litres] of barley seed.

In ancient times the shekel was simply a unit of weight of about 11 g (⅓ oz), and it is thought that it originally referred to the weight of barley. Later it became a coin's name as well, and today in Israel it refers only to that country's currency.

Barley was harvested in April or May, depending on the weather and the farm's position. The size of the barley harvest in about 950 BC can be judged from words that King Solomon sent to King Hiram of Tyre as part of his request for wood and workers to help build his new temple:

2 CHRONICLES

CH. 2, VV. 8-10

My men shall work with yours to provide me with plenty of timber, because the temple I build must be large and magnificent. I will give your servants, the woodsmen who cut the timber, 20,000 cors [c. 4,400 kilolitres/120,000 bushels] of ground wheat, 20,000 cors of barley, 20,000 baths [c. 440 kilolitres/95,000 gallons] of wine and 20,000 baths of olive oil.

The quantity of food and drink that Solomon promised was much needed – the end of Chapter 2 records that he ordered 153,000 men to be the work force! By New Testament times it is recorded that a worker gets 'three quarts (about a litre) of barley for a day's wage' (Revelation ch. 6, v. 6).

Barley produces a nutritious food. Although it was considered an inferior grain to wheat, its wholemeal flour was and is much used in cooking. After the death of Joshua, Israel fell into the hands of the Midianites. Their home territory was flanking the eastern arm of the Red Sea. It was where Moses fled after he had killed the Egyptian (Exodus ch. 2). After nine years of oppression, Gideon was leader of the desire to be rid of the Midianites:

Now the camp of Midian lay below him in the valley. During the night the Lord said to Gideon, "Get up, go down against the camp, because I am going to give it into your hands. If you are afraid to

JUDGES

CH. 7, VV. 8-14

attack, go down to the camp with your servant
Purah and listen to what they are saying …"
Gideon arrived just as a man was telling his friend
his dream. "I had a dream," he was saying. "A
round loaf of barley bread came tumbling into
the Midianite camp. It struck the tent with such
force that the tent overturned and collapsed."
His friend responded, "This can be nothing other
than the sword of Gideon son of Joash, the Israelite.
God has given the Midianites into his hands."

Indeed He had. With only 300 men, Gideon routed the enemy, who fled. Revelations by dreams are often mentioned in the Old Testament. This dream's imagery is particularly apposite because the barley of the loaf is worth only half as much as wheat, and is a good symbol for Israel whose numbers were far fewer than the enemy. Gideon would have found much comfort in what he overheard.

In contrast a splendid, peaceful story which includes the barley loaf, is found in all four Gospels, although only St John names what sort of bread is involved. A large crowd has followed Jesus up a mountain. Jesus asks his disciples as a test, how are the people to be fed:

ST JOHN

CH. 6, VV. 7-13

Philip answered him, "Eight months' wages would
not buy enough bread for each one to have a bite!"
Another of the disciples, Andrew, Simon Peter's
brother, spoke up. "Here is a boy with five barley
loaves and two small fish, but how far will they go
among so many?"
Jesus said, "Make the people sit down." There was
plenty of grass in that place, and the men sat down,
about five thousand of them. Jesus then took
the loaves, gave thanks, and distributed to those
who were seated as much as they wanted.
He did the same with the fish.
When they had all had enough to eat, he said to
the disciples, "Gather the pieces that are left over.

Let nothing be wasted."
So they gathered them and filled twelve baskets
with the pieces of the five barley loaves left over by
those who had eaten. 〰

Barley loaves were cheap, the food of the poor. The miraculous feeding of the crowd – 5,000 men; women and children were not counted – was a splendid preface to the meeting later that Jesus had with his disciples when he told them that:

 ST JOHN
CH. 6, VV. 34-35

"you ate the loaves and had your fill. Do not work
for food that spoils, but for food that endures to
eternal life, which the Son of man will give you ..."
"Sir," they said, "from now on give us this bread."
Then Jesus declared, "I am the bread of life. He
who comes to me will never go hungry, and he who
believes in me will never be thirsty." 〰

This declaration by Jesus is the first of seven I AM descriptions by Jesus of himself, all recorded only in St John's gospel. The crowd and the disciples did not understand it. They still thought Jesus was talking about real bread. With "I am the bread" Jesus is echoing God's words telling Moses His name, "I AM WHO I AM" (Exodus ch. 3, v. 14), and in so saying Jesus is stating His own divinity and putting Himself on a collision course with the authorities; He left the crowd grumbling and arguing, "How can this man give us his flesh to eat?" The disciples said it was a hard lesson, but Simon Peter finally admitted on their behalf, "You have the words of eternal life. We believe and know that you are the Holy One of God." (St John ch. 6, vv. 68, 69). The Christian today finds this is still a hard lesson to understand, and he or she needs the faith of Peter to be able to say "I believe".

One of the most well-known stories in the Old Testament is the story of Jacob's young son, Joseph. Thanks to Andrew Lloyd Webber's musical *Joseph and the Technicolour Dreamcoat*, thousands of people, young and old, know something of the story, which is a big feature of the Bible's first book, Genesis. The story begins when:

WHEAT

> *Joseph, a young man of seventeen was tending the flocks with his brothers … Now Israel [i.e. Jacob, his father] loved Joseph more than any of his other sons because he had been born to him in his old age; and he made a richly ornamented robe for him. When his brothers saw their father loved him more than any of them, they hated him and could not speak a kind word to him.*
>
> *Joseph had a dream, and when he told it to his brothers, they hated him all the more. He said to them, "Listen to this dream I had: we were binding sheaves of corn out in the fields when suddenly my sheaf rose and stood upright, while your sheaves gathered round mine and bowed down to it."*

 GENESIS
CH. 37, vv. 2-8

His brothers said to him, "Do you intend to reign over us?" As a result of their jealousy they plotted to kill him, but instead, when they were all out tending their flocks, they sold him to Midianite traders who were on their way to Egypt. That at last brings us firmly to the resolution of the very important story about Joseph's dream about sheaves of corn. In Egypt, Joseph interpreted dreams for servants and Pharaoh, and was rewarded by the Pharaoh who put him in charge of all Egypt, which meant he controlled the saving of the wheat harvest throughout the country:

GENESIS
CH. 41, v. 49

> *Joseph stored up huge quantities of grain, like the sand of the sea. It was so much he stopped keeping records because it was beyond measure.*

The rest of the family story and its happy ending is told in Genesis chh. 42–47.

Joseph's dream 'corn' is really wheat; in English the word 'corn' has for centuries referred to any form of grain; nowadays, the word technically should refer to maize (*Zea* spp.), a cereal from the Americas. Wild *emmer* and *einkorn* forms of wheat (*Triticum* spp.) were first cultivated in the Fertile Crescent. Archaeological evidence of *einkorn* wheat has been discovered in Jordan dating back to 7500–7300 BC, and there is evidence for *emmer* wheat in Iran as old as 9600 BC. The genetics of wheat are complicated. It is self-pollinating and cultivation has resulted in the creation of several domestic forms. In Joseph's time wheat was harvested in early summer, about a month after barley. Harvesting was labour intensive. The farmer would grasp a handful of stalks in his left hand, cut them fairly high up with a sickle held in the right hand, and bind them into sheaves. Corn was left growing in difficult-to-reap corners of the field; that and seed fallen to the ground was left for the gleaners, as is told in the story of Ruth. She was a Moabite woman over 3,000 years ago, who asked her widowed Israelite mother-in-law if she could go in the fields and pick up the leftover grain. The rest of the story is an intimate, delightful glimpse into family life (Ruth ch. 1–4).

The farmer was still left with much to do. Sheaves were taken to a threshing floor in carts or on the backs of asses. This floor was a circular patch of hard, dry, flat ground, which was usually the common property of the village. A common method of threshing was to scatter the sheaves and drive a hard wood sledge pulled by an ox or two over them. The grain was now freed from the husk but was mixed with broken straw and chaff. This was thrown into the air from a shovel – a process called winnowing – whereupon the heavier grain fell and the chaff blew away. Very often a final cleaning was achieved by sieving the grain. Several times the prophet Isaiah uses images of wheat farming to illustrate what is happening to the Jews, especially when he tells them this message from God:

🙊 ISAIAH
CH. 28, VV. 23-29

Listen and hear my voice;
pay attention and hear what I say.
When a farmer ploughs for planting,
does he plough continually?
Does he keep on breaking up and
harrowing the soil?
When he has levelled the surface.
Does he not sow caraway and scatter cummin?
Does he not sow wheat in its place,
barley in its plot, and spelt in its fields?
His God instructs him
and teaches him the right way.
Caraway is not threshed with a sledge,
nor is a cartwheel rolled over cummin;
caraway is beaten with a rod, and cummin with a stick.
Grain must be ground to make bread;
so one does not go on threshing it for ever. 🙊

Melon

Spelt is another form of ancient wheat. There is scientific evidence that it was a hybrid of *emmer* and a wild grass which grew in the Middle East long before Wheat (*Triticum aestivum*) as we know it appeared. Despite the Bible reference, some commentators do not believe spelt was cultivated in Mesopotamia, but is the result of the confusion with *emmer* wheat. Isaiah's poetic parable is thought to be saying that although God must punish Israel, his actions will be as well controlled as a good farmer's would be.

Finally the precious crop was stored. If done carefully, it would keep for several years, as Joseph found in Egypt. Underground, bottle-shaped silos were dug, or the grain was kept in big earthenware jars. Modern excavations at Jericho have found millet, barley and lentils in round clay bins, which had been stored over 5,000 years ago! The harvest is still a time celebrated by people of many faiths. Christians, in both country and city churches, sing harvest songs, such as *We plough the fields and scatter/The good seed on the land*. City churchgoers sing it even though no-one in the city has ever ploughed a field or harvested the ripe corn. Believers are mindful of the debt they owe to God for the bountiful food that *is* provided. It may well have come from the supermarket, but someone at home or abroad has produced it.

Isaiah's message from God quoted above mentions other crops apart from grain. Vegetables and herbs were a part of home life but a vegetable garden as we know it was likely only at the houses of the wealthy. Notwithstanding that, the Israelites when they were in Egypt, were familiar with several such foods and angrily remarked to Moses early in their escape from Pharaoh:

 NUMBERS
CH. 11, vv. 4-5

If only we had meat to eat! We remember the fish we ate in Egypt at no cost – also the cucumbers, melons, leeks, onions and garlic.

Many years later Isaiah tells the sinful Israelites that the desolation they have suffered from invaders over at least two centuries has resulted in Jerusalem being no more defensible than a:

 ISAIAH
CH. 1, v. 8

*shelter in a vineyard,
like a hut in a field of melons,
like a city under siege.*

The owner of a vineyard often built a tower there and employed a watch-keeper to protect his crop. The word for 'melons' here is translated as 'cucumbers' in some versions of the

Bible. The Melon (*Citrullus lanatus*) was once common in ancient times in Egypt, is now grown widely in Palestine and marketed throughout the land.

When Ahab was king of Israel, the northern kingdom, from 874–853 BC, he said to Naboth in Samaria, "Let me have your vineyard to use for a vegetable garden". Naboth refused, but Ahab's wife Jezebel plotted against Naboth, had him stoned to death for reportedly having cursed God and the king, and so gained the vineyard. But Ahab would have nothing to do with his wife's evil desires (1 Kings ch. 21). At the end of His life, when Jesus came finally to Jerusalem, He taught the crowds and harangued the hypocrisy of the Saducees and Pharisees, using a homely image to make His point:

ST MATTHEW
CH. 23, V. 23
(ALSO ST LUKE CH. 11, V. 42)

Woe to you, teachers of the law and Pharisees, you hypocrites! You give a tenth of your spices – mint, dill, and cummin. But you have neglected the more important matters of the law – justice, mercy and faithfulness. You should have practised the latter, without neglecting the former.

Jesus doesn't criticize observing the law, but the hypocrisy of following some parts and not others. We sometimes do just that today, following the liturgy of our favourite church service but failing to love our neighbours as ourselves.

The stories clearly show that vegetables and spices were an important part of life. They were all used to season food. Mint (*Mentha* spp.) is a perennial with many forms worldwide, including Peppermint (*M. piperita*) and Spearmint (*M. spicata*), which are the two species most widely used in the temperate world in cooking. The leaf is used, fresh or dried, in Europe and the Middle East with lamb, or to make mint tea. Dill (*Anethum graveolens*) is related to celery. Its leaves are aromatic and are widely used in Europe, the Middle East and Asia to flavour fish, pickles and soup. It is an annual herb. Cummin (*Cuminum cyminum*) is an annual plant in the parsley family, and the seasoning is obtained by using the dried or

MINT

crushed seeds, giving an earthy flavour. It was a feature of Ancient Egyptian cooking and later part of Jewish, Greek and Roman cuisine. Shortly before King David went to battle with Absolom who had conspired against him, the people he was with:

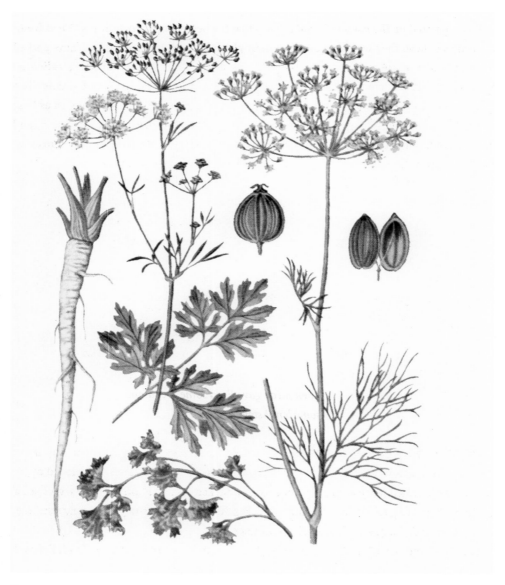

DILL

2 SAMUEL
CH. 17, VV. 28-29

brought wheat and barley, flour and roasted grain, beans and lentils, honey and curds, and cheese from cows' milk [see p. 151] for David and his people to eat.

It is suggested in *The Jewish Virtual Library* that the beans were Broad Beans (*Vicia faba*); historians believe they were one of the earliest plants to be cultivated, and became part of mankind's diet in the eastern Mediterranean around 6000 BC. The Lentils (*Lens culinaris*) are edible seeds in the pea family, known as pulses. They have been eaten by humans since Neolithic times. Lentils were also one of the first crops cultivated in the Middle East as long as 13,000 years ago! Modern science has discovered they are a rich source of protein, and were undoubtedly a common food of the poorer people, judging from the few references we have in the scriptures. The most famous Bible story which speaks of Lentils is:

GENESIS
CH. 25, VV. 29-34

when Jacob was cooking some stew, Esau came in from the open country, famished. He said to Jacob [his brother], "Quick, let me have some of that red stew! I'm famished!" (That is why he was also called Edom).

Jacob replied, "First sell me your birthright."
"Look I am about to die" Esau said.
"What good is the birthright to me?"
But Jacob said, "Swear to me first." So he swore an oath to him, selling his birthright to Jacob. Then Jacob gave Esau some bread and some lentil stew.

LENTILS

When the lentil pods are boiled they turn reddish-brown, still remembered by many today in the words of the *Authorized Version* as 'a mess of pottage'. Later, encouraged by his mother who treated Jacob as her favourite son, he tricked his old, blind father into giving the eldest son's blessing to himself, causing much family friction. The story is a timely reminder even today of the dangers of parental favouritism.

One of the most exotic references to plants is in *Song of Songs*. The Lover says to his Beloved:

OTHER CROPS | 59

> *Your plants are an orchard of pomegranates and*
> *choice fruits, with henna and nard,*
> *nard and saffron,*
> *calamus and cinnamon,*
> *with every kind of incense tree,*
> *with myrrh and aloes*
> *and all the finest spices.*

SONG OF SONGS
CH. 4, VV. 13-14

The substances named are a mixture of fruit (already discussed), cosmetics and incense. Saffron was a luxury item, this time derived from the Saffron Crocus (*Crocus sativus*), a cultivated form of the wild Crocus of the Mediterranean region, and used for flavouring and the orange-yellow colouring of food. The lilac-to-mauve flowers are harvested in the autumn. It is such an expensive spice, because saffron powder is produced from freshly picked Crocus flowers – but only the red stigmas or 'threads' from the centres of the flowers are collected for the best product. Today 450 g (1 lb) of dry Saffron needs a harvest of 50,000–75,000 flowers, or a kilogram requires 110,000–170,000! The Beloved was a wealthy woman to have a farm and workers to be able to grow enough Crocuses for her saffron.

SAFFRON CROCUS

Calamus or Sweet Flag (*Acorus calamus*) probably originated in Asia but is found widely in Europe. It is a wetland plant, whose scented leaves and even more strongly scented rhizomes (the plant's rootstock), have been used for many centuries in medicines, perfumes and as substitutes for ginger, cinnamon and nutmeg – which may be some of the spices suggested by the Lover. We know it was used as early as 1300 BC in Ancient Egypt. Its mention by the Lover may be most closely linked to its long having been a symbol of love, which was very much at the heart of his song. Elsewhere, it is mentioned once each in Isaiah (ch. 43, v. 24) and Jeremiah (ch. 6, v. 20), where it is most probably referred to as an ingredient in an anointing oil. Jeremiah clearly lists it as an imported item into Israel – 'from a distant land' – not a local product, again suggesting it was a luxury item for the Beloved to be growing.

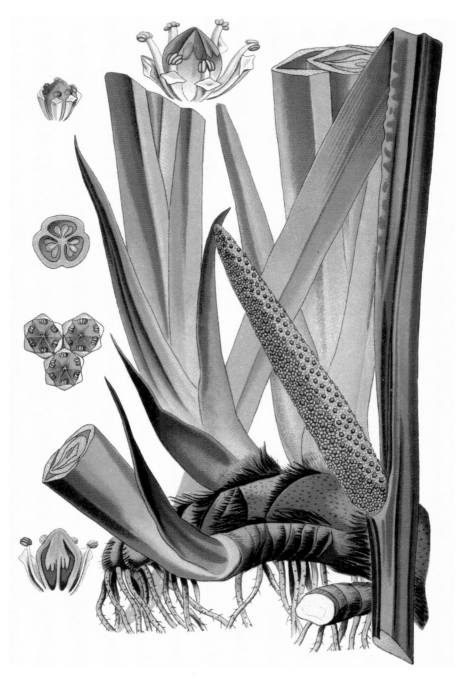

Calamus or Sweet Flag

The writer of Proverbs also mentions 'myrrh, aloes and cinnamon' together in one quotation (Proverbs ch. 7, v. 17). Myrrh is a gum commonly harvested from a small thorny tree, *Commiphora myrrha*, native to the southern Arabian peninsula and north-east Africa. A related species, *Commiphora gileadensis*, grows in the eastern Mediterranean. Myrrh was

ALOE

used as an ingredient in the embalming of bodies in Ancient Egypt, in sacred incense in the Temple, in the holy anointing oil (Esther ch. 2, v. 12) and as a drug to dull the senses. To Christians the last use is most famously mentioned as one of the three gifts given to Jesus at His birth by the Three Wise Men (St Matthew ch. 2, v. 11), and then in the drink offered to Him by the Roman soldiers at His Crucifixion (St Mark ch. 15, v. 23). How many Wise Men came is not stated; we say 'three' because they brought three gifts.

Aloes are succulent plants of many species, widespread across Africa, the Middle East and Asia. *Aloe vera* is the species most commonly used in herbal medicines, to produce a soothing ointment, to treat wounds and in the making of soap, and is still used in the pharmaceutical industry today. The ancient Greeks and Romans, for example, used it to treat wounds. After the death of Jesus, Joseph of Arimethea took the body with Pilate's permission to inter it in the tomb that Joseph had prepared for himself, as was the custom. Nicodemus, who was another secret follower of Jesus and was the same man who had visited Jesus by night (St John ch. 3), accompanied Joseph:

ST JOHN
CH. 19, vv. 39-40

Nicodemus brought a mixture of myrrh and aloes, about seventy-five pounds [about 34 kilos]. *Taking Jesus' body, the two of them wrapped it, with the spices, in strips of linen. This was in accordance with Jewish burial customs.*

The quantity of spices was unusually large, such as might have been used at a royal funeral, of King Asa of Judah (2 Chronicles ch. 16, v. 14), for example. It shows how important the two men considered Jesus to be. To them He *was* indeed the King, but as Jesus said to Pilate at His trial, His kingdom was not of this world. Pilate did not understand that nor did the soldiers who made the crown of thorns and yelled sarcastically, "Hail king of the Jews!" When He was put on the cross, the notice 'Jesus of Nazareth, King of the Jews' was nailed to the cross too. The Jewish authorities protested, saying it should say that He claimed to be the king. But Pilate refused to change it. Jews today are still waiting for the Messiah, the king; and around the world today there are many people of other faiths who scorn Christ as did the Roman soldiers, kill those who do follow Him, and destroy Christian churches. Christ's gospel of love is hard to believe in, and hard to stay true to when one does believe – witness the fact that Joseph and Nicodemus worked secretly – and not long after the Christ's resurrection, Stephen was stoned to death because he refused to deny Christ.

The spices tell a mixed story of human love of others, love of one's own appearance, our love of tasty food, and our care for the sick and injured and dead. From small seeds and flowers great things grow when nurtured with the love of God.

There are many references to clothes and furnishings like curtains made of linen, in both the New and Old Testaments. Linen is a textile made from the fibres of the Flax plant (*Linum usitatissimum*). Garments made from it are good for keeping you cool and staying fresh in hot weather. When Pharaoh put Joseph in charge of the country 'He dressed him in robes of fine linen' (Genesis ch. 41, v. 42); the palace of Xerxes, who reigned in Persia from 486–465 BC, had a garden in which were 'hangings of white and blue linen' (Esther ch. 1, v. 6); all four Gospel writers describe Jesus' body being wrapped in linen; and the cloth was held in such high esteem that John records 'That fine linen stands for the righteous acts of the saints' (Revelation ch. 19, v. 9). Egyptian mummies were wrapped in linen; and linen cloth was found in the first half of the 20th century in Cave One during the excavations of the Dead Sea scrolls. The earliest recorded production of the cloth is in Egyptian records 4,000 years old. The fibres are obtained by soaking the stems in water which loosens the fibres (called 'retting'), then the woody part of the stalk is removed by crushing the plant between rollers ('scutching') and the fibres are combed, spun into yarn, and finally woven.

Finally we will consider the sacred plant Hyssop (*Hyssopus officinalis*), a member of the mint family, and native

HYSSOP

FLAX PLANT

to southern Europe and the Middle East. It is used as an aromatic herb and as a medicine. Its first mention is a dramatic one in the time leading up to the Israelites leaving Egypt:

EXODUS
CH. 11, vv. 31-13

Then Moses summoned all the elders of Israel and said to them, "Go at once and select the animals for your families and slaughter the Passover lamb. Take a bunch of hyssop, dip it into the blood in the basin and put some of the blood in the top and on both sides of the door frame. Not one of you shall go out of the door of his house until morning. When the Lord goes through the land to strike down the Egyptians he will see the blood on the top and sides of the door frame and will pass over the doorway, and he will not permit the destroyer to enter your houses and strike you down."

Later, a law was made which said that a person who had suffered an infectious disease could be cleansed by sprinkling him or her with blood from a slaughtered bird, which was on the tip of a sprig of Hyssop (Leviticus ch. 14, vv. 1–9). The writer of *The letter to the Hebrews* firmly reminds his readers of this use of the Hyssop stick when he writes about the blood of Christ, and declares:

HEBREWS
CH. 9, v. 9

In fact, the law requires that nearly everything be cleansed with blood, and without the shedding of blood there is no forgiveness.

Today Christians celebrate this in the sacrament of Holy Communion, the Eucharist, when they eat the bread and drink the wine, the body and blood of Christ, in remembrance of His taking the sins of the world on his shoulders (1 Corinthians ch. 11, vv. 23–26).

CHAPTER IV

FLOWERS

There is much in the news nowadays about the land around the world and what grows on it – or does not grow, because we have ruined the ground with pesticides, or have built on it, or caused severe erosion through deforestation. It is of concern to many people. In the United Kingdom the authorities are increasingly aware of the way that wild flowers show us the state of health of the land, and are helping landowners to farm profitably in an eco-friendly way. But not all the people involved will believe that God had a hand in what they do, when He declared:

GENESIS
CH. 1, vv. 26-31

"Let us make man in our image, in our likeness, and let them rule over the fish of the sea and the birds of the air, over the livestock, over all the earth. And over all the creatures that move along the ground." So God created man in his own image ... Then God said, "I give you every seed-bearing plant on the face of the whole earth and every tree that has fruit with seed in it" ... And God saw all that he had made, and it was very good.

There is much debate about that gift of all those plants, and the statement which followed:

GENESIS
CH. 2, v. 15

The Lord God took the man and put him in the Garden of Eden to work it and take care of it.

Many people of different faiths *do* believe they have to *take care of* the land and what grows there. That is how they 'rule over' it. They have lived long on the land, and have grown to realise that as a family or tribe or nation they have lived long because they do realise how best to look after the farm or the forest. If they are greedy or careless, they will grow hungry, or starve and die. St Peter wrote a letter in the early 60s AD, which he addressed to the gentile Christians in particular who were spread across Asia Minor. In their time of Roman

Darnel

oppression, he reminded them of the steadfastness of God when they feel downtrodden by quoting words that the prophet Isaiah had said to the Israelites centuries before:

For you have been born again, not of perishable

1 PETER *seed, but of imperishable, through the living and*

CH. 1, vv. 23-25 *enduring word of God. For,*

& *All men are like grass,*

ISAIAH *and all their glory like the flowers of the field;*

CH. 40, vv. 6-8 *the grass withers and the flowers fall,*

but the word of the Lord stands for ever.

Let us consider in some detail the 'grass' and the 'flowers' that the writers record on and off throughout the Bible. We dismiss many plants in the countryside, and more so if they in our gardens, as 'weeds'. The word is used repeatedly in the Parable of the Weeds which is recorded only in St Matthew's gospel:

Jesus told them another parable: "The kingdom of

heaven is like a man who sowed good seed in his

field. But while everyone was sleeping, his enemy

came and sowed weeds among the wheat, and went

ST MATTHEW *away. Then the wheat sprouted and formed ears,*

CH. 13, vv. 24-28 *then the weeds also appeared.*

The owner's servants came to him and said, "Sir,

didn't you sow good seed in your field? Where then

did the weeds come from?"

"An enemy did this", he replied.

His disciples didn't understand the parable and Jesus had to explain it to them. He was the landowner, the Devil was the enemy, the field was the world and the weeds were the sons of the Devil; and at harvest time, the end of the age, angels will weed out the kingdom and throw the evil into the fire, and the righteous will be gathered to be with their father. The old translations used the word 'tares' for the weeds, and many commentators now believe the weed was the plant Darnel (*Lolium temulentum*), also known as Cockle. It grows where wheat is grown, and looks so like it that it is also called False Wheat. Not until the ears appear can the two be easily separated: ripe wheat ears are brown, Darnel's are black. Darnel can be infected with a fungus. If these seeds are eaten they can cause a drunken nausea or even death. The scientific name *temulentum* means 'drunk'. Jesus really did know about the problems of harvest-time. His message would have been much more dramatic to his hearers than to us when we hear just the word 'weeds'.

MENORAH

For centuries before the Star of David became a well-known Jewish symbol, the seven-branched lampstand called the 'menorah' was the best-known symbol. Its form was described by God to Moses as part of God's instructions for the building of the Tabernacle and its furnishings:

≈ EXODUS
CH. 25, VV. 31-32

Make a lampstand of pure gold and hammer it out, base and shaft; its flower-like cups, buds and blossoms shall be of one piece with it. Six branches are to extend from the sides of the lampstand – three on one side and three on the other. ≈

SAGE

Although the cups for the oil lamps on top of each branch are described as being 'like almond flowers', there is an ancient Jewish tradition that suggests that the shape of the complete lamp resembles the flower they call 'moriah' or 'morvah', and which botanists know as Jerusalem Sage (*Salvia hierosolymitana*), a native plant of the area, in the same family as mint. Two other flowers, Pungent or Dominican Sage (*Salvia dominica*) and Land of Israel Sage (*Salvia palaestina*) have a similar, branched shape, so all three may have had an influence on the design. One commentator has said they are 'menorahs growing wild'.

Jerusalem Sage is drought resistant, and lights up the stony land in spring with its pink flowers. The lampstand came to

PAPYRUS

represent The Tree of Life in Jewish tradition, promising fertility. All three sages grow in the 400-acre reserve called Neot Kedumim – the Biblical Landscape Reserve in Israel. This series of gardens is being specially constructed to show all the plants named in the Bible. The 'menorah plants' all grow in a terrace at the top of the hill. The gardens' emblem is the Caper (*Capparis spinosa*), which is mentioned only once in the Bible – if you believe some translations, such as this one from the *British Revised Version*:

ECCLESIASTES   *... the grasshopper loses its spring,*
CH. 12, v. 5   *and the caper berry has no effect;*

But although this is clearly the flower named in the Septuagint (Greek), the Vulgate (Latin) and a few modern English versions, most translations, such as the widely read *New International Version*, the *Revised King James* and the *Good News Bible,* all have the word 'desire' instead of 'the caper berry'. The founders of the gardens believe the caper's productivity, strength and endurance are all what is meant by modern 'Israel'. However, in Biblical times the plant was believed to have aphrodisiac properties, so we are back to 'desire' again!

The heart-warming story of how Joseph saved Egypt and his family from starving in a time of famine by carefully storing the grain from several good harvests (see pp. 51–53), is followed by tales of the oppressed lives the Israelites lived in Egypt until they were led to freedom by Moses. His life began very dramatically after Pharaoh had shown concern about the number of Israelites being born in his kingdom. Pharaoh decreed that all newborn boys should be thrown into the Nile. Moses' mother managed to hide him for three months after his birth but then put him in a papyrus basket coated with tar and pitch and put it in the reeds on the banks of the Nile.

The happy result was that he was rescued by an Egyptian princess. Historians believe she may have been Hatshepsut, 'Foremost of noble ladies', who became queen and later Pharaoh, builder of an amazing temple near Luxor, and died in 1458 BC. Even more intriguing for the purpose of this chapter is the description of the basket, which gives us the well known story 'Moses and the bullrushes'. What plants are mentioned? Papyrus and reeds. Papyrus (*Cyperus papyrus*) is a wetland sedge which grows along the Nile and was used by the ancient Egyptians as far back as the fourth millennium BC. The pith of Papyrus stems was soaked, cut into lengths, beaten and fixed together to make a sheet which when dry could be written on, then rolled into a scroll to be stored. Documents as old as 2500 BC have been discovered at a site on the Red Sea coast. Even more interesting is the prophecy:

> *ISAIAH*
> CH. 18, vv. 1-2
>
> *Woe to the land of whirring wings*
> *along the rivers of Cush* [ancient Ethiopia],
> *which sends envoys by sea*
> *in papyrus boats over the water.*

The stems and leaves of Papyrus were durable enough to be woven into a strong basket, or even a boat. The mention of reeds is a mistranslation. The writers of the *Authorized Version* were not familiar with vegetation along the Nile and translated the ancient word with the name of a plant which seemed right to them – the general word 'reeds' and the Bullrush or Reedmace (*Typha latifolia*), both familiar sights by English rivers. However, the Hebrew word here, *gime,* really refers to Papyrus. The idea of Moses in the Bullrushes really stuck in the modern mind due to the frequent depiction of the story by artists showing English Bullrushes, despite there being many paintings from previous centuries which clearly show the plant native to the Nile, Papyrus.

Another problem in translation is that concerned with the mentions of thorns, briers, thistles, nettles and brambles. Modern scholarship is certain about the identity of some but not all. For example, the prophet Isaiah had comforting words for the Israelites in exile:

> *ISAIAH*
> CH. 55, vv. 6 & 12–13
>
> *Seek the Lord while he may be found;*
> *call on him while he is near.*
> *You will go out in joy*
> *and be led forth in peace;*
> *the mountains and hills*
> *will burst into song before you,*
> *and all the trees of the field*
> *will clap their hands.*
> *Instead of the thornbush will grow the pine tree.*
> *And instead of briers the myrtle will grow.*

As we have seen (see p. 14) the thorns could be those on the Acacia bush. But the Brier (also spelt 'briar') is also mentioned by Job, who in his anger, curses his land:

> *JOB*
> CH. 31, v. 40
>
> *then let briers come up instead of wheat*
> *and weeds instead of barley.*

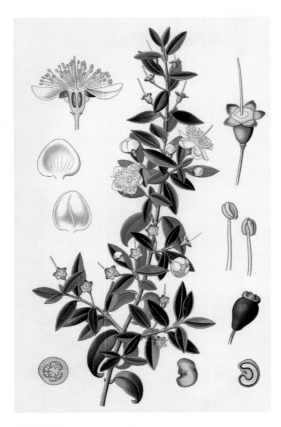

MYRTLE

The *Zondervan Encyclopedia of the Bible* records that the Hebrew word here, *hoah*, is one of several in the language used for thorns. Job's curse appears in the *Revised Standard Version* of the Bible as 'foul weeds'. The *Encyclopedia* wonders whether the plant could be the Palestinian Nightshade (*Solanum incanum),* which is a common weed in the Jordan valley, and native to the Middle East. It is a member of the nightshade family and is related to the two species found in Britain; it has poisonous berries. It certainly is not the wild Sweetbriar Rose (*Rosa rubiginosa*) of our hedgerows. Whatever plant was originally meant, and whichever English word is in the translation, it is clear that a plant with disagreeable features is meant because of the contrast made between it and Myrtle *(Myrtus communis).* This latter has aromatic leaves and white flowers from which spices and medicines were made, it is named as one of God's blessings and its twigs are still used in the ritual of the Feast of the Tabernacles (see pp. 18–21).

Thorns feature prominently in one of Jesus' parables, recorded in St Matthew ch. 13, St Mark ch. 4 and St Luke ch. 8: 'Parable of the Sower. Thistles (*Centaurea* spp.) are also used as an image of misery. Several species, which are common on rough ground, I have seen on the hills around Galilee. The *Good News Bible* translates the Job passage we have just read as '... then instead of wheat and barley, may weeds and thistles grow', and three times Isaiah warns that the Israelites will be punished by God, as when he says for example, 'The wickedness of the people burns like a fire that destroys thorn-bushes and thistles' (Isaiah ch. 9, v. 18). The *NIV* translation is not so precise; the fire 'consumes briers and thorns'. Amaziah, King of Judah, was at war with Jehoash, King of Israel, in the late 700s BC, and:

2 CHRONICLES
CH. 25, VV. 17-18

When Amaziah king of Judah consulted his advisors, he sent this challenge to Jehoash son of Jehoahaz, son of Jehu, king of Israel: "Come, meet me face to face".
But Jehoash king of Israel replied to Amaziah king of Judah: "A thistle in Lebanon sent a message to a cedar in Lebanon, 'Give my daughter to my son in marriage.' Then a wild beast in Lebanon came along and trampled the thistle underfoot."

BRAMBLE

We have already read (pp. 15–17) how great in many respects the Cedar Tree was. How insignificant a thistle would appear beside such a tree! Jehoash, the wild beast, did rout the Amaziah thistle in battle shortly afterwards. The meaning is clear in the references to a thistle, as anyone can appreciate who has been out walking and has brushed against the prickly stems of a thistle, or tried to pick one of its lovely flowers, and cried aloud with pain!

Despite the ministrations of his Comforter, Bildad, Job bemoans the way he is treated by the young sons of men who were forced to live rough:

⤳ JOB
CH. 30, v. 7
(AUTHORIZED VERSION)

Among the bushes they brayed;
under the nettles they were gathered together. ⤳

There are no Nettles (*Urtica dioica*) in modern translations, just men 'huddled in the undergrowth'. It is hard to imagine anyone lying in a bed of Nettles without suffering greatly!

The last of the prickly plants is the Bramble (*Rubus fruticosus*), at least that is the species we affectionately know and harvest wild or cultivated as the Blackberry. There are about 2,000 varieties so we cannot be sure which St Luke was referring to here in recording these words of Jesus:

⤳ ST LUKE
CH. 6, vv. 43-45

No good tree bears bad fruit, nor does a bad tree
bear good fruit. Each tree is recognized by its own
fruit. People do not pick figs from thorn-bushes, or
grapes from briers. A good man brings forth good
things out of the good stored up in his heart, and
an evil man brings evil things out of the evil stored
up in his heart. For out of the overflow of his heart
his mouth speaks. ⤳

The *Good News Bible* boldly says 'bramble bushes' not 'briers'. Jesus uses images from the countryside several times. He was often alone in the hills so would have been familiar with briers or brambles. The ones He knew well and believed his audience would recognize, were not ones which gave good fruit like we know, but were plants that were useless as food, so underlining His comparison of good and evil, which is what He was preaching about.

The last group of plants comprises those we would acknowledge as flowers as opposed to weeds. Jesus' well-known words to His disciples set the scene:

ST LUKE
CH. 12, vv. 27-29

Consider how the lilies grow. They do not labour or spin. Yet I tell you, not even Solomon in all his splendour was dressed like one of these. If that is how God clothes the grass of the field, which is here today, and tomorrow is thrown into the fire, how much more will he clothe you, O you of little faith!

The *Concordance to the Good News Bible* lists nearly 40 references for 'flower', but few to the name of a flower. We immediately run into translation problems again. For example, the prophet Hosea at the end of his book tells of God's promise to bring a blessing to Israel:

HOSEA
CH. 14, vv. 4-5 (NIV)

I will heal their waywardness and love them freely, for my anger has turned away from them. I will be like the dew to Israel; he will blossom like a lily.

But *NIV's* 'blossom like a lily' becomes 'blossom like flowers' in the *Good News*.

In the Old Testament the Hebrew name *shushan* or *shoshan*, i.e., 'whiteness', was used as the general name for several plants common to the eastern Mediterranean, such as the tulip, iris, anemone, gladiolus and buttercup. Some interpret it, with much probability, as denoting the Water-lily (*Nymphoea lotus*) or lotus. Its flowers are large, and they are white with streaks of pink. They supplied models for the ornaments of the pillars of Solomon's temple (1 Kings ch. 7, v. 19). Some commentators strongly argue that the word, both in the Old and New Testaments, denotes liliaceous plants in general, or if one genus is to be selected, that it must be the genus *Iris*, which is 'large, vigorous, elegant in form and gorgeous in colouring'.

The lilies spoken of in the New Testament by St Luke were recorded by the Greek word, *krinia*. They may be the Scarlet Martagon (*Lilium chalcedonicum*) or Red Turk's-cap Lily, which Balfour in his *Plants of the Bible* (1886) says 'comes into flower at the season of the year when our Lord's sermon on the mount is supposed to have been delivered. It is abundant in the district of Galilee; and its fine scarlet flowers render it a very conspicuous and showy object, which would naturally attract the attention of the hearers.'

A different point-of-view was held by the Rev. Tristram who wrote *The Natural History of the Bible* (1867) in which he says, 'Of the true "floral glories of Palestine", the Pheasant's Eye (*Adonis palestina*), the Persian Buttercup (*Ranunculus asiaticus*) and the Anemone (*Anemone coronaria*), the last named is however, with the greatest probability regarded as the 'lily of the field' to which our Lord refers. Certainly,' continued the Rev. Tristram who had spent much time there, 'if, in the wondrous richness of bloom which characterizes the land of Israel in spring, any one plant can claim pre-eminence, it is the Anemone, the most natural flower for our Lord to pluck and seize upon as an illustration, whether walking in the fields or sitting on the hill-side. The White Water-lily (*Nymphcea alba*) and the Yellow Water-lily (*Nuphar lutea*) are both abundant in the marshes of the Upper Jordan, but have no connection with the lily of Scripture.'

Whatever the flower, Jesus is pointing out that Solomon's glory is artificial, organized and dressed by Solomon himself, whereas the disciples – and we – should cast all our care upon the Lord.

The Beloved and the Lover in their duet say – or sing – to each other:

Beloved
I am a rose of Sharon,
SONG OF SONGS *a lily of the valleys.*
CH. 2, VV. 1-2 *Lover*
Like a lily among thorns
is my darling among the maidens.

Sharon is the coastal plain south of Mt Carmel. 'Rose of Sharon' first appeared in English in the 1611 *Authorized King James Bible*, and has since become a name around the world for many different beautiful flowers. For example, a *Hibiscus* Rose of Sharon is the national flower of South Korea! Various scholarly attempts have been published to say which 'rose' it is; they are all certain it is not the Rose (*Rosa* sp.) we know. It has been suggested it is a mistranslation of a general Hebrew word for crocus; it might be the red Mountain Tulip (*Tulipa Montana*) which is common in the hills around Sharon; or the most likely is that it is the white Sea Daffodil (*Pancratium maritimum*), which is common around the shores of the Mediterranean, and which I have seen flowering there. The lovers seem to be trying to outdo each other with compliments. I do like the thought that the loving couple are both picturing the woman as white, which is the colour for purity; that may be emphasized in the man's choice of 'lily' – the impressive Madonna Lily (*Lilium candidum*) perhaps, which is native to the area?

SEA DAFFODIL

We can be a little more sure with Broom, of which there are several species. The most likely one in Psalm 120 and Job ch. 30 is Mediterranean Broom (*Genista linifolia*), a shrub growing up to 2 m (6 ft) with tough green leaves and yellow, pea-like flowers. In the same reference in Job we read of the men who mocked him:

> ⌇ JOB   *In the brush they gathered salt herbs,*
> CH. 30, V. 4   *and their food was the root of the broom tree.* ⌇

There is wide agreement that the salt herbs were a species of Saltwort or Glasswort (*Salicornia* sp.), which grows by the shore and is tolerant of salt water. The one we know in Europe has long been known as good to eat, raw or cooked. It has a high salt content. We call one species Samphire or St Peter's Herb. Job knew of it as a commonly sought, natural food.

Perhaps the most unusual plant recorded in the Bible is in the story of Jacob's wife, Rachel. When she learns that her sister, Leah, is pregnant she is jealous. Then:

> ⌇ GENESIS   *During wheat harvest, Reuben went out into the fields and found some mandrake plants, which he brought to his mother Leah. Rachel said to Leah, "Please give me some of your son's mandrakes." But she said to her, "Wasn't it enough that you took away my husband? Will you take my son's mandrakes too?"*
> CH. 30, VV. 14-16
> *"Very well," Rachel said, "he can sleep with you tonight in return for your son's mandrakes."*
> *So when Jacob came in from the fields that evening, Leah went out to meet him. "You must sleep with me," she said. "I have hired you with my son's mandrakes." So he slept with her that night.* ⌇

GLASSWORT

Jacob had fled to his uncle Laban after he had tricked his own father and obtained his brother's birthright. He fell in love with Rachel, Laban's beautiful daughter, but was tricked himself by Laban and found himself married to Leah, the older, weak-eyed sister. In the end, half of Jacob's twelve sons were by Leah. Read Genesis chapters 28–30 for the whole story!

An Israelite in theory could have several wives. The Bible explicitly allowed a man to have

Madonna Lily

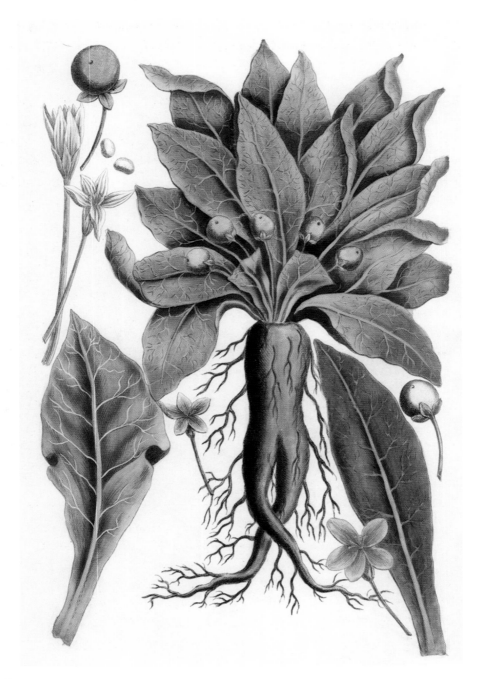

MANDRAKE

more than one wife. God gives Moses a law which talks about making sure the first wife still gets the same resources and attention now that she's not the only one, Exodus ch. 21, vv. 10–11. So in Jacob's time, what happened to him and Leah was not an improper act as many will see it today.

The Mandrake is the common name for several species of the genus *Mandragora* of the nightshade family. The most likely species here is *Mandragora officinarum*. The forked, fleshy roots of the plant resemble the lower part of the human body and, if eaten, were supposed to help a woman become pregnant. The Hebrew word for it is *doo-dah'-ee*, meaning literally 'love producing'. The roots are hallucinogenic and narcotic. The Beloved we have just read about is not such an innocent as she seemed earlier when she says to her Lover:

> *Let us go early to the vineyards*
> *to see if the vines have budded,*
> *if their blossoms have opened,*
>
> SONG OF SONGS   *and if the pomegranates are in bloom –*
> CH. 7, vv. 12-13   *there I will give you my love.*
> *The mandrakes send out their fragrance*
> *and at our door is every delicacy, both new and old,*
> *that I have stored up for you, my lover.*

Two amazing soap-opera stories by our standards. Life carries on much as it has done for centuries.

INSECTS

I t is widely believed that James, the brother of Jesus, was the author of the letter in the New Testament bearing his name. He wrote it in the early 60s AD for Christians from the Jews of 'the twelve tribes scattered among the nations'. He spends much of chapter 3 exhorting his readers to 'tame their tongues', to make sure that they use it to praise rather than to curse. He emphasizes this by saying:

 JAMES
CH. 3, VV. 7-8

All kinds of animals, birds, reptiles and creatures of the sea are being tamed and have been tamed by man, but no man can tame the tongue. It is a restless evil, full of deadly poison.

Leaving James' lesson aside (but not forgotten!), we note interestingly that there are no insects in that list. Yet bee-keeping – apiculture – was practised by the ancient Egyptians, and archaeologists discovered hives at a dig at Rehov in the Jordan valley dating back to 900 BC. It is hard to believe that James did not know about hives of bees or colonies of wild bees. Bees and honey are mentioned so often in the scriptures, one of the earliest has become proverbial:

EXODUS
CH. 3, VV. 7-8

The Lord said, "I have indeed seen the misery of my people in Egypt ... So I have come down to rescue them from the hand of the Egyptians and to bring them up out of that land into a good and spacious land, a land flowing with milk and honey ...

From the *Authorized Version* onwards the description of a good country to live in has been said to be 'flowing with milk and honey', in other words, it lacks nothing in the way of nutritious and sweet food. That is where the Israelites were now living, in Canaan. Long after the Exodus, King Saul fought the Philistines, who were on the run, but before the Israelites pursued them Saul ordered his men not to eat anything before evening came:

WESTERN HONEY BEES

*So none of the troops tasted food.
The entire army entered the woods, and there was
honey on the ground. When they went into the
woods, they saw the honey oozing out, yet no-one
put his hand to his mouth, because they feared the
oath. But Jonathan had not heard that his father
had bound the people with the oath, so he reached
out the end of the staff that was in his hand and
dipped it into the honeycomb.*

It becomes clear that Saul is not fit to be a leader. His grasp of military tactics was poor. He learns that Jonathan has apparently disobeyed him and threatens to kill him, but is saved by the appeals of his own soldiers. 'Honey on the ground' sounds curious. Wild bees build a nest of honeycomb in the treetops. If one had fallen, Jonathan could certainly have poked his staff into it. Or it might be that the retreating Philistines dropped their food as they fled, which led Jonathan to say:

1 SAMUEL
CH. 14, V. 30

*How much better it would have been if the men
had eaten today some of the plunder they took
from their enemies.*

An even more extraordinary story concerns Samson. At his wedding feast he told a riddle to the 30 companions he had been given as was the custom among the Philistines:

"Tell us your riddle," they said. "Let's hear it."
He replied.
*"Out of the eater, something to eat;
out of the strong, something sweet."*
For three days they could not give the answer.

Samson's new wife pleads with him for the answer. On his way for his first visit to her he had killed a young lion. Later he had gone past it again, found a nest of bees in it and ate some of the honey, which in true Hebrew fashion meant that he was defiled, having touched a dead body. Eventually he gives in and tells her the answer. She of course tells her kinsmen, and:

Before sunset on the seventh day
[the deadline Samson had given the
men to answer the riddle]
the men of the town said to him,
"What is sweeter than honey?
What is stronger than a lion?"
Samson said to them,
"If you had not ploughed with my heifer,
You would not have solved my riddle."

JUDGES
CH. 14, V. 18

WESTERN HONEY BEES

We usually think of Samson as a hero. Although he did give those who had solved the riddle the clothes he promised if they won, they were clothes he obtained by striking down and stripping 30 men of Ashkelon, one of the five principal cities of Philistine; this, and his description of his wife, are two facts that reveal a very different character. Compared with the story where we learn that he lost his strength as a child because of the evil doings of Delilah (who was in the pay of the rulers of the Philistines) which result in the 'hero's' death, he appears now as a *much* less appealing man, hardly a hero – he disobeyed his parents, failed to follow Hebrew law, rudely referred to his wife, angered the men of Ashkelon, was infatuated with Delilah, and above all 'he did not know that the Lord had left him' (Judges 16, v. 20). And it all began with honey!

Though domestic hives of bees are not mentioned in the Bible. It is clear that honey was important because of the large number of references to it, so it is reasonable to assume honey was harvested easily from colonies in hives. Western Honey Bees (*Apis mellifera*) of Europe, Asia and Africa were domesticated at least 4,000 years ago by the Egyptians.

Most often the honey is praised for its sweetness, either literally as in 'What is sweeter than honey?' (Judges ch. 14, v. 18), or in a comparison such as that describing the commands of God as 'sweeter than honey, than honey from the comb' (Psalm 19, v. 10). There are seven proverbs which name honey (in Proverbs chh. 5, 16, 24 (two), 25 (two) and 27), all naming honey in a way which gives advice for good living. Modern dieticians are campaigning today about our eating too much sugar.

The locust is arguably the most important insect in the Bible, where it features prominently in many stories. Two species in particular occur in Palestine, the Desert Locust (*Schistocerca gregaria*), widely distributed in North Africa, the Middle East and India, and the Migratory Locust (*Locusta migratoria*), found from Africa to Australia.

The Israelites, led by Moses, were desperate to leave Egypt where they lived as slaves, but Pharaoh refused to let them go. Moses appeals to God who promises help, which comes in the form of dreadful natural disasters – the Nile stained red like blood, plagues of frogs, gnats, flies, diseased livestock, boils, hail, darkness and penultimately, locusts:

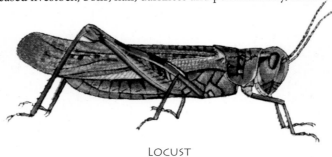

LOCUST

So Moses stretched out his staff over Egypt, and the Lord made an east wind blow across the land all that day and all that night. By morning the wind had brought the locusts; they invaded all Egypt and settled down in every area of the country in great numbers. Never before had there been such a plague of locusts, nor will there ever be again. They covered all the ground until it was black. They devoured all that was left after the hail – everything growing in the fields and the fruit on the trees. Nothing green remained on tree or plant in all the land of Egypt. ⪥

The fact that the east wind blew the locusts to Egypt suggests they were Migratory Locusts. The Israelites were released, but only after the last disaster, the death of every first-born son, including the Pharaoh's.

It is believed that the prophet Joel lived in the 9th century BC when 'The word of the Lord' came to him, warning the people of Judah of trouble ahead, and calling on them all to repent:

DESERT LOCUST

~~ JOEL

CH. 1, vv. 1-4

Hear this, you elders;
listen all who live in the land.
Has anything like this ever happened in your days
or in the days of your forefathers?
Tell it to your children,
and let your children tell it to their children,
and their children to the next generation.
What the locust swarm has left
the great locusts have eaten;
what the great locusts have left
the young locusts have eaten;
what the young locusts have left
other locusts have eaten. ~~

Locusts are grasshoppers! There are ten Hebrew words used in the scriptures to signify locust. The insect is solitary in its first immature, flightless forms, until certain suitable conditions change it behaviourally to a gregarious insect, when it forms large bands, then swarms 'without number' as flying adults. Carried on the wind these swarms travel far. The writers of Exodus, the writer of psalm 105 referring to locusts and grasshoppers, and Joel were right. A swarm might cover several square kilometres/miles, and number millions of insects, each devouring its own weight of food in a day, thousands of tons of precious human

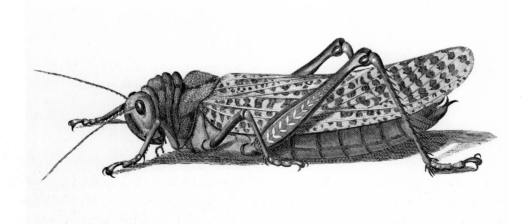

LOCUST

crops, causing appalling devastation to valuable farmland, such as happened in Pharaoh's Egypt. Swarms still occur today, as in Palestine in March to October 1915, and autumn 2004, both of which caused great hardship. Several organizations around the world today monitor the threat from swarms and endeavour to control the swarm by spreading insecticide over it from the air, or on the vegetation they are heading towards.

In the New Testament locusts are mentioned as forming part of the food of John the Baptist :

 ST MARK
CH. 1, V. 6

John wore clothing made of camel's hair,
with a leather belt round his waist,
and he ate locusts and wild honey.

By the Mosaic law, locusts were reckoned to be 'clean', so that he could lawfully eat them. Locusts are prepared as food in various ways. Sometimes they are pounded, mixed with flour and water and baked into cakes; 'sometimes boiled, roasted, or stewed in butter, and then eaten'. They were eaten in a preserved state by the ancient Assyrians as is shown in a carving nearly 3,000 years old, of a waiter bringing several dozen fixed on skewers to a feast – locust kebabs!

The writers of the Bible can be forgiven for not knowing the source of silk, although they surely knew it as a high-value cloth. When Ezekiel was describing the unfaithfulness of Jerusalem he described her as if she were a prostitute dressed in silk (*Good News Bible,* chapter 16, v. 13), and at the end of the Bible, John says of Babylon (his code word for Roman domination):

 REVELATION
CH. 18, VV. 11-12

the merchants of the earth will weep and mourn
over her because no-one buys her cargoes any
more – cargoes of gold, silver, precious stones and
pearls, fine linen, purple*, silk and scarlet cloth

(*Purple was a valuable dye.)

He certainly knew that silk was imported by the Romans. We know now that silk is produced by the Silkworm, so it is worth mentioning here. Silk is produced by the caterpillar of the Silk Moth (*Bombyx mandarina*) and its domesticated form (*Bombyx mori*). The caterpillars feed on

Mulberry leaves, and the silk is obtained from its cocoon. It was first domesticated 5,000 years ago in China. Silk was exported westwards along the Silk Road, a UNESCO-designated World Heritage Site, and was particularly developed in the period 200 BC – 200 AD.

The ant, one of over 10,000 known species in the family *Formicidae*, has come down to us in a proverb, which I can remember being told me as a boy many years ago:

∽ PROVERBS
CH. 6, vv. 6-8

Go to the ant you sluggard;
consider its ways and be wise!
It has no commander,
no overseer or ruler,
yet it stores its provisions in summer
and gathers its food at harvest. ∽

Even after all those years I still find 'sluggard' a rare but interesting word, and was surprised and pleased that the *NIV* still uses it. The effect of the *Good News* version is not nearly so dramatic:

Lazy people should learn a lesson from the way
ants live. They have no leader, chief or ruler,
but they store up their food during the summer,
getting ready for the winter.

Ants are certainly not lazy. They are very social insects that live in highly structured societies in nests that they construct in trees, underground or in ground-level mounds. They do have a 'chief' known as a 'queen', but her role is only to produce thousands of eggs, which are tended and guarded by 'workers', wingless females. Males have one function – to mate with the queen after which they die. The colony survives thanks to the perfect sharing of work, which is genetically built into each ant. They do not have to think about it; they just do it. Ants do collect food very busily. Some species 'milk' aphids and scale insects of their sweet secretion called 'honeydew'; various species of Leafcutter Ants (*Atta* and *Acromyrmec* spp.) cut leaves, take them to the nest, and feed on the fungus which then grows on the cut leaves. Also in Proverbs we read:

∽ PROVERBS
CH. 30, v. 25

Ants are creatures of little strength,
yet they store up their food in the summer ... ∽

SILK MOTH

Several species collect and store grain for the winter. But the writer was not as accurate with regard to ants' strength. For their size ants are very strong. Watch ants for any length of time, and you'll witness some remarkable feats of strength. Tiny ants, marching in lines, will haul food, grains of sand, and even small pebbles back to their colonies. They can lift objects 50 times their own body weight. Their muscles – particularly neck muscles, because they lift the weight by holding it in their jaws – are thicker in proportion than those of larger animals or even humans.

Yet another saying we still hear today was originally said by the prophet Isaiah 3000 years ago:

 ISAIAH
CH. 51, VV. 7-8

Do not fear the reproach of men
or be terrified by their insults.
For the moth will eat them up like a garment;
the worm will devour them like wool.

Isaiah was quite right in observing that the moth's caterpillar really does the damage, and its favourite food is wool. Moths can be a serious pest, and heated homes allow them to breed all year round. The adult moth does not feed and dies after it has mated. The moth was an image used by Jesus centuries later:

ST MATTHEW
CH. 6, VV. 19-21

Do not store up for yourselves treasures on earth,
where moth and rust destroy, and where thieves
break in and steal. But store up for yourselves
treasures in heaven, where moth and rust do not
destroy, and where thieves do not break in and
steal. For where your treasure is, there your heart
will be also.

The prophet was suggesting that troublesome men would be hurt themselves, but Jesus was using the Clothes Moth (*Tineola bisselliella*) as an image to help people realise that material wealth does not last, and worse still, it means the person is 'worshipping' wealth not God.

Jesus preached on the topic of riches several times, especially the repeated message in St Luke chapter 16 where we read of the Prodigal or Lost Son who squandered his inheritance, the rich man who commended his shrewd manager, and the parable of the rich man who went to hell and Lazarus who begged by his gate who went to heaven when he died. The Bible very firmly teaches that wealth really is destroyed by moth and rust.

ORIENTAL HORNET

In many warm and tropical lands people who have a meal out of doors are often pestered by wasps or even its larger relative, the Hornet (*Vespa* spp.). It is recorded early on the story of the Jews' entry into the Promised Land. The Hebrew word *tsir'ah* is used, meaning 'stinging', as when God says:

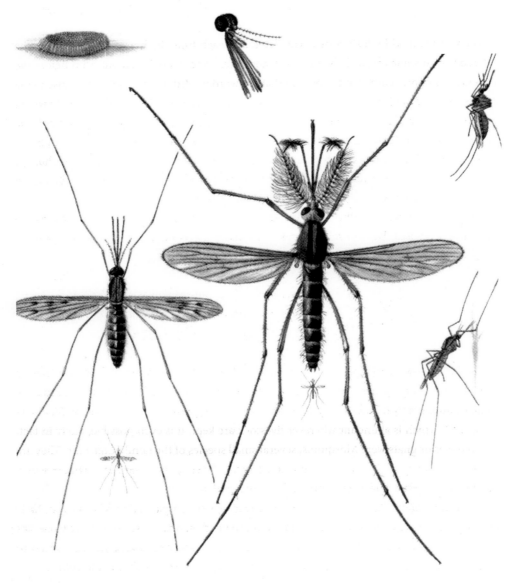

MALARIA MOSQUITO

EXODUS

CH. 23, VV. 27-28

I will send my terror ahead of you and throw confusion into every nation you encounter. I will make all your enemies turn their backs and run. I will send the hornet ahead of you to drive the Hivites, Canaanites and Hittites out of your way.

The word is used by Joshua two years later, and each time the hornet is mentioned, the reference is to some means by which the Canaanites were to be driven out from before the Israelites. Commentators have supposed that the word is used in a metaphorical sense as the symbol of some panic which would seize the people as a 'terror of God', and not that it would be thought that real hornets would be the attackers. In Palestine the most likely species is the Oriental Hornet (*Vespa orientalis*), differing from European Hornets (*Vespa crabro*) by being larger in size. They form a colony underground. It has been recorded they do attack human beings very fiercely, and the furious attack of a swarm of hornets drives cattle and horses to madness, and has even caused the death of the animals.

Other plagues which afflicted Egypt were of gnats and flies. The former became so numerous because 'All the dust throughout the land of Egypt became gnats' (although older translations say 'lice'), and:

EXODUS

CH. 8, VV. 17 & 25

Dense swarms of flies poured into Pharaoh's palace and into the houses of his officials, and throughout Egypt the land was ruined by the flies.

We don't know which species of gnat was involved. They are mostly tiny insects that do form large mating swarms, especially at dusk. They might even have been bloodsucking midges, which carry diseases. The flies could well have been the Stable or Barn Fly (*Stomoxys calcitrans*), which is abundant wherever livestock are kept. It is even possible, likely in fact, that the flies or gnats were Mosquitos, several small species of the family *Culicidae*. They are most well known as the carrier of malaria (*Anopheles* sp.), and breed in stagnant water; people living by the Nile were in prime mosquito habitat.

In the early days of the flight from Egypt, the Israelites complained to Moses about their lack of food. As we have read (pp. 24–26) God provided manna, which they were to eat but not save any overnight – they did and next morning 'it was full of maggots and began to smell' (Exodus 16, v. 20). But a later word from God explained how they could collect twice

SPIDER AND ANTS

as much on the sixth day of the week, bake it, boil it and save whatever was left for the Sabbath next day, the day of rest, when they were not supposed to work. 'So they saved it until morning, as Moses commanded, and it did not stink or get maggots in it' (Exodus 16, v. 24).

It is fascinating what details are *not* in a story, which we readers today would like to know – were the insects Mosquitos? – and what details *are* in the history – maggots in the manna!

Yet another disagreeable insect in the Bible is recorded solely in the story of David's troubled life with King Saul. Saul is looking for David, to kill him.

They meet and David says to Saul:

> 1 SAMUEL *The king of Israel has come out to look for a flea –*
> CH. 26, v. 20 *as one hunts a partridge in the mountains.*

David, at the same time that he is not afraid to picture himself as a tiny flea, suggests that King Saul is making a fool of himself by chasing him, an innocent man, with a great hunting party. The speech works, and Saul blesses David, says he will do great things and triumph, and they go their separate ways. There are about 2,000 species of flea worldwide, all wingless insects. They are external parasites, living by sucking the blood of animals and birds. David, as a soldier living rough, almost certainly knew at first hand the Human Flea (*Pulex irritans*), well-named because its bite does leave a very irritating, red mark; besides causing the itching, they are also the carriers of several diseases.

Two animals end this chapter, which are not insects though they are invertebrates (i.e. they have no backbone or spine). The first is the spider, a member of the order of *Arachnids* which have eight legs compared to an insect's six. There are over 40,000 species worldwide. Bildad, one of Job's friends, believes Job has upset God; that is why he is suffering:

> *Such is the destiny of all who forget God;*
> *so perishes the hope of the godless.*
> JOB *What he trusts in is fragile;*
> CH. 8, vv. 13-15 *what he relies on is a spider's web.*
> *He leans on the web, but it gives way;*
> *he clings to it, but it does not hold.*

When we have brushed unexpectedly into a web we can appreciate its fragility. On the face of it, Bildad's illustration is good. Modern science, however, has discovered that spider's silk has the tensile strength of steel. It is not as strong as steel but has a similar breaking point before it snaps. Many species of bird know this and use spiders' web to bind materials together in the construction of their nests – hummingbirds and the European Chaffinch are good examples.

When Ezekiel was 30, the age when a young man could enter the priesthood, he heard a call from God:

⮞ EZEKIEL
CH. 2, VV. 3-6

Son of man, I am sending you to the Israelites, to a rebellious nation that has rebelled against me … Do not be afraid of them or their words. Do not be afraid, though briers and thorns are all around you and you live among scorpions. ⮜

Jesus often taught about prayer. He urged his followers to be bold or persistent in prayer, not just to pray on special occasions:

SCORPION (LEFT) AND SPIDER

ST LUKE
CH. 11, vv. 9-12

So I say to you: Ask and it will be given to you;
seek and you will find; knock and the door will be
opened to you. For everyone who asks receives;
he who seeks finds; and to him who knocks,
the door will be opened.
Which of you fathers, if your son asks for a fish,
will give him a snake instead? Or if he asks for
an egg, will give him a scorpion?

Both appeals name the scorpion, an eight-legged creature in the same class of animals as spiders, *Arachnida*. There are over a 1,000 known species throughout the world, mostly in warm climes. All are predatory, but only a few are poisonous; these are naturally the ones which humans are particularly aware of, as Moses reminded the Israelites:

DEUTERONOMY
CH. 8, v. 15

[God] led you through the vast and dreadful
desert, that thirsty and waterless land,
with its venomous snakes and scorpions.

The writer of Revelation was well aware of the Scorpion's sting in the tip of its tail when he told in his vision that the godless people would suffer agony 'like that of the sting of the scorpion' (Revelations ch. 9, v. 5). All the references to the scorpion are when the writer or speaker wants to make sure that the audience is very aware of the unpleasantness or weakness of a choice in which God does not feature.

It is a shame that the writers of the Bible told us only about insects which they think of as symbols of disaster, or which produce good food, or are an illustration of a good way to live. There are no dragonflies or butterflies, two glories of God's insect creation. But we must be grateful nevertheless, that the insects remind us of the sweetness of honey, the industry of the ant and the wisdom of not storing up treasure on earth.

CHAPTER **VI**

REPTILES

The English language is rich in synonyms – witness this list of words, which, on the face of it, all describe the same creature – snake, serpent, adder, viper, cobra and asp. Then when we come to read about these reptiles in the Bible, we discover that at least nine Hebrew words for this animal are listed in Strong's *Exhaustive Concordance*, which compound the problem for translators of finding the correct English word. The roots of the Hebrew words describe the animal's behaviour, so the context of the word will help the translators get the best sense.

One could be forgiven for thinking that Satan, the Devil, had got among the text to upset things just as he did in the Garden of Eden, in the form of a serpent (or snake or adder, even different editions of *NIV* do not agree!). The woman is persuaded by the snake to eat fruit from the forbidden tree. She also gives it to Adam, so that they both have their eyes opened to good and evil. When God finds out about this, he says to the snake:

GENESIS
CH. 3, VV. 1-20

"Because you have done this, cursed are you above all livestock and all wild animals! You will crawl on your belly and you will eat dust all the days of your life. And I will put enmity between you and the woman, and between your offspring and hers; he will crush your head, and you will strike his heel."
To the woman he said, "I will make your pains in childbearing very severe; with painful labour you will give birth to children. Your desire will be for your husband, and he will rule over you."
To Adam he said, "Because you listened to your wife and ate fruit from the tree about which I commanded you, You must not eat from it, cursed is the ground because of you; through painful toil you will eat food from it all the days of your life. It will produce thorns and thistles for you, and you

COBRA (BELOW)

will eat the plants of the field. By the sweat of your
brow you will eat your food until you return to
the ground, since from it you were taken; for dust
you are and to dust you will return."
Adam named his wife Eve, because she would
become the mother of all the living. ∾

The snake (serpent) is a symbolic creature in many cultures across the world, from Ancient Egyptian to Norse to Greek to Indian to Australian mythology. Adam and Eve's meeting with it has resulted in the Jewish and Christian faiths seeing the episode as a way of describing Mankind's fall from God's grace, of the power of temptation and the source of that power, and learning the difference between good and evil. God's different punishments for Adam and Eve and the snake are all ways of explaining in those days basic questions of life and death – Adam will have to struggle to find food to live all his life, childbirth for Eve will be painful, the struggle between man and the snake is the ongoing fight between good and evil.

We have already read how the Israelites complained to Moses about the lack of food in the wilderness (p. 24) and God sent them manna. There was another miracle too:

∾ NUMBERS
CH. 21, VV. 4-9

The people grew impatient on the way, they spoke
against God and against Moses, and said, "Why
have you brought us up out of Egypt to die in the
desert? There is no bread! There is no water!
And we detest this miserable food!"
Then the Lord sent venomous snakes among them;
they bit the people and many Israelites died. The
people came to Moses and said, "We sinned when
we spoke against the Lord and against you. Pray
that the Lord will take the snakes away from us."
So Moses prayed for the people.
The Lord said to Moses, "Make a snake and put it
on a pole; anyone who is bitten can look on it and
live." So Moses made a bronze snake and put it up
on a pole. Then anyone who was bitten by a snake
and looked at the bronze snake, he lived. ∾

Horned Viper

St John reminds his readers of this event when he retells Jesus' teaching to Nicodemus about being born again and says:

NILE CROCODILE

ST JOHN
CH. 3, v. 14-15

Just as Moses lifted up the snake in the desert,
so the Son of man must be lifted up, that everyone
who believes in him may have eternal life.

The first hearers of John's gospel would have been well aware of the new life that God gave the Israelites in the desert, and may well have been startled by Jesus stating that He was going to be lifted up, on a cross as John later recorded, and believers in Christ's message would be 'born again', and they 'may have life, and have it to the full' (St John ch. 10, v. 10).

Moses features in two other snake stories. After he had spoken to God in the burning bush, God told him He would help him to persuade the elders of the Israelites to go with him to Pharaoh to persuade him to let the Israelites leave Egypt:

EXODUS
CH. 4, vv. 1-3

Moses answered, "What if they do not believe
me or listen to me and say, 'The Lord did not
appear to you'?"
Then the Lord said to him,
"What is that in your hand?"
"A staff," he replied.
The lord said, "Throw it on the ground."
Moses threw it on the ground and it became
a snake, and he ran from it.

Moses is told to pick it up. He does and it becomes a staff again. No matter that God says that this miracle will persuade the elders to let him go to Pharaoh, Moses says he is 'slow of speech and tongue … Oh Lord, please send someone else to do it.' (vv. 10 and 13). God is angry but insists that Moses joins forces with his brother Aaron. Together they do visit Pharaoh, perform the miracle before Pharaoh who commands his magicians to do:

EXODUS
CH. 7, vv. 11-13

the same things by their secret arts. Each one threw
down his staff and it became a snake. But Aaron's
staff swallowed up their staffs. Yet Pharaoh's heart
became hard and he would not listen to them, just
as the Lord had said.

It was only after all the plagues (see p. 88) that the Israelites were released. Even today God-fearing people make excuses when God asks them to do a task just like Moses did, instead of believing that God will help.

Snakes generally are linked to descriptions of mortal threats:

(see p. 88)

<table>
<tr><td>≈ PSALM
91, vv. 1-13</td><td>He who dwells in the shelter of the Most High
will rest in the shadow of the Almighty.
I will say to the Lord, "He is my refuge and my fortress,
my God, in whom I trust ...
You will not fear the terror of night,
nor the arrow that flies by day …
You will tread upon the lion and the cobra;
you will trample the great lion and the serpent. ≈</td></tr>
</table>

The Psalmist carefully balances the emphatic list of dangers, with the power of God's help which will positively help the believer. There are clearly two Hebrew words in the original, which have taxed translators ever since, hence the two English words. The quotation above is from *NIV*; the Authorised Version of 1611 finishes verse 13 with 'the lion and the adder' and 'the young lion and the dragon', and the *Good News* speaks of 'lions and snakes' and 'fierce lions and poisonous snakes'. If 'cobra' is right it could be the Egyptian or Hooded Cobra (*Naja haje*), which is found across North Africa and the Israelites would have got to know it in Egypt, but Rev. Tristram recorded it as rare in Palestine. He does list over two dozen species of snakes in the region, including several species of Vipers (*Vipera* spp.).

That name is used to describe snakes in several stories, perhaps most dramatically here when St Paul was shipwrecked on his way to Rome:

<table>
<tr><td>≈ ACTS OF
THE APOSTLES
CH. 28, vv. 1-5</td><td>Once safely on shore, we found out that the island
was called Malta. The islanders showed us unusual
kindness. They built a fire and welcomed us all
because it was raining and cold. Paul gathered a pile
of brushwood and, as he put it on the fire, a viper,
driven out by the heat, fastened itself on his hand.
When the islanders saw the snake hanging from his
hand, they said to each other, "This man must be a</td></tr>
</table>

THORNY-TAILED AGAMA

murderer; for though he escaped from the sea,
Justice has not allowed him to live." But Paul shook
the snake off into the fire and suffered no ill effects. ⬙

The islanders then thought he was a god! The snake's identification as a viper goes back to the *Authorised Version*, but the *Good News* says vaguely 'snake'. The Psalmist also refers to poisonous snakes:

⬙ PSALM
58, vv. 4-5

[Unjust rulers'] venom is like the venom of a snake,
like that of a cobra that has stopped its ears,
that will not heed the tune of the charmer,
however skilful the enchanter may be. ⬙

NILE MONITOR

It is fascinating to read that all that time ago the Hooded Cobra was the snake charmer's chosen beast as it is today. St Paul was convinced that we were all sinners and needed faith in Jesus Christ to become righteous. He described people's sinfulness as:

 ROMANS
CH. 3, V. 13

Their throats are open graves;
their tongues practise deceit.
The poison of vipers is on their lips.

The *Authorised Version* and the *New King James* speak of 'asps' not vipers and the *Good News* refers to 'snake's poison'. Asp is the anglicized word from Latin *aspis,* which in ancient Egyptian and Roman times was used to describe any of several poisonous snakes. Famously it became the killer of Cleopatra of Egypt. There is a reference to England's only poisonous snake, the Adder, in Jacob's prophetic blessing to his sons:

 GENESIS
CH. 49, V. 17
(AUTHORISED VERSION)

Dan will be a serpent by the way, an adder on
the path, that biteth the horse's heels, so that
his rider shall fall backwards.

The treachery of the tribe of Dan is told later in Judges chapter 18. *NIV* says 'serpent' and 'viper' and the *Good News* once again vaguely talks about 'snake' and 'poisonous snake'. In English 'adder' and 'viper' are synonymous, and the 17th century translators can be forgiven for using 'adder' because they would not have had experience of other poisonous snakes, and their readers – and many readers today – would certainly understand a poisonous snake was meant. This reference has even been thought to mean the Horned Viper (*Cerastes cerastes*), which is widespread across the deserts of North Africa and the Middle East. It is easily recognized by the horn over each eye and its 'side winding' movement.

After so many references to the disagreeable nature of snakes, the following statement may seem to be a surprise, coming as it does in Jesus' instructions to his disciples:

 ST MATTHEW
CH. 10, V. 16

I am sending you out like sheep among wolves.
Therefore be as shrewd as snakes and as innocent
as doves.

The first sentence clearly hints at the fact that Jesus knew that Israel's allegiance to God was nominal. The second sentence sounds like a proverbial expression, and it is Jesus' way of exhorting the disciples to use every way possible to protect themselves from those who would persecute them, and is an echo of a saying of the rabbis, 'The holy and blessed God said to the Israelites, "Towards Me the Israelites are uncorrupt like doves, but towards the Gentiles they are as cunning as serpents."' We are back to the Garden of Eden.

In our own churches and churchyards are Celtic crosses dating from the early Middle Ages which have snakes carved on them, such as the Saxon example of c.1000 AD in the Church of the Holy Cross, Ramsbury, Wiltshire. The snake sheds its skin as it grows, and seems to be born again. It is not surprising therefore, that the reptile became a symbol for rebirth, which is a key part of Christian belief as we have seen. Sometimes the snake appears to be eating its own tail, and so is depicting infinity, the circle of life, eternal life. The same symbolism can be seen on many bishops' staffs (croziers) in the carving of a snake's head for the crook at the top.

When you read The Bible and come across a reference to 'snake', try to look at several translations; then you will have the best understanding of the way the writer wants you to think of the mention of the beast – a natural danger or symbolic of treachery or the embodiment of evil or symbolic of a Christian belief or just a wild animal.

The laws in the book Leviticus include lists of foods which may be eaten (clean) and foods which may not (unclean). The distinction goes back to the story of Noah (Genesis ch. 7), and the main reason for the division into two classes of food, was to preserve the sanctity of Israel as God's chosen people. One list in particular adds to our list of reptiles:

 LEVITICUS
CH. 11, VV. 29-30

Of the animals that move about on the ground, these are unclean to you: … any kind of great lizard, the gecko, the monitor lizard, the wall lizard, the skink and the chameleon.

Various commentaries admit that the precise identity of some of the animals is uncertain. The 'great lizard' has been thought to be the Nile Crocodile (*Crocodylus niloticus*), the second largest living reptile in the world; old mature males can grow up to 5.5 m (18 ft) long. It is widespread in fresh waters throughout Africa and formerly was found as far north as the Nile delta, so really could have been known to the Israelites when they were in Egypt. However, the *International Standard Bible Encyclopedia*, after careful argument considers

LIZARD

Mediterranean Chameleon

the six reptiles in the list to be Thorny-tailed Lizard, monitor, gecko, true lizard, skink and Chameleon; The McClintock and Strong *Biblical Cyclopedia* has a similar list of species but does not agree with which Hebrew word goes with each lizard!

These species are probably: Rough-tailed Rock or Thorny-tailed Agama (*Stellagama stellio*) (formerly *Lacerta stellio*), found throughout the Middle East and common in farms and gardens; the Desert Monitor (*Varanus griseus*), 2 m (6 ft) long and found widely in the Middle East, including Palestine, or the equally long Nile Monitor (*Varanus niloticus*), a native of Egypt; the Mediterranean Gecko (*Hemidactylus turcicus*) or the Fan-footed Gecko (*Ptyodactylus gecko*) are possibly the geckos; it would be good to think that the 'true lizard' is the Be'er Shaeva Fringe-fingered Lizard (*Acanthodactylus beershebensis*), found only in south-central Israel in the Negev desert; but a small wall lizard is much more likely, such as the Lebanon Lizard (*Phoenicolacerta laevis*), which is common; the skink may be the Ocellated Skink (*Chalcides ocellatus*), one of many species found in sandy places or the Sandfish Skink (*Scincus scincus*); finally there is no doubt that the Common or Mediterranean Chameleon (*Chamaeleo chamaeleon*) is part of the Leviticus list.

There are over 20 species of lizard recorded in Palestine, so what is remarkable is the fact that centuries before the discipline of zoology and the naming of species, the Israelites had noticed the differences in the lizards and had names for the most obvious ones. The Bible has only two references to lizards, in Leviticus, and the writer of Proverbs who counted 'four things on earth are small', one of which was 'a lizard [which] can be caught with the hand, yet it is found in king's palaces' (Proverbs ch. 30, v. 28). In warm countries like Palestine, geckos are small, familiar sights indoors, clinging to ceiling or wall by means of their specially adapted toes, covered in tiny hairs, which enable them even to walk up a window. They are most probably the lizards the writer had seen, even in a palace.

For all their importance in the 'unclean food' list, there are no other lizard references in modern translations, although the *Authorised Version* tried hard with the Hebrew word *tannin,* which modern scholars are still struggling with. There we read that 'dragons and owls will honour' Isaiah, Job thinks he is 'a brother to dragons' and Jeremiah believes Jerusalem will become 'a den of dragons'. Modern translations refer to 'jackals' every time because the context suits that prowling animal, and we do not have the superstitious belief in dragons that existed in the 17 century.

Two other reptiles are worthy of note. The second great plague that was inflicted on the Egyptians was a plague of frogs, most particularly the Egyptian or Dotted frog (*Rana punctata*), so named because its brown colour is covered with green spots:

GODDESS HEQET

EXODUS
CH. 8, VV. 6-11

Aaron stretched out his hand over the waters of Egypt, and the frogs came up and covered the land. … Pharaoh summoned Moses and Aaron and said, "Pray to the Lord to take the frogs away from me and my people, and I will let you go to offer sacrifices to the Lord". … Moses replied, "It will be as you say, so that you know there is no-one like the Lord our God. The frogs will leave you and your houses …"

The frog was a symbol of life and fertililty because they were so plentiful after the annual Nile floods that nourished the soil.

But Pharaoh did not keep his word until eight more plagues had struck. The plagues were to show that the Hebrews' god was a living God, and the Egyptian gods were worthless. The frog plague was a judgement against Heqet, the Egyptian frog-headed goddess of birth. The writer of Revelation (ch. 16, v. 13) names frogs in one of his visions as 'evil spirits' who will lead the people to support the cause of evil; so frogs are an image there in keeping with their being 'unclean'.

The second reptile features in God's mysterious question to Job:

JOB
CH. 41, VV. 1-2 & 7-8

*Can you pull in the Leviathan with a fishhook
or tie down his tongue with a rope?
Can you put a cord through his nose
or pierce his jaw with a hook?
…
Can you fill his hide with harpoons
or his head with fishing spears?
If you lay a hand on him,
you will remember the struggle and never do it again.*

Most commentators think the Nile Crocodile is the animal here. It is a beast the Israelites would have certainly got to know during their time in Egypt. The description clearly is referring to an animal that lives in water, and would have been seen by fisherman who would have understood is strength and ferocity. The Leviathan is surely a crocodile.

Egyptian or Dotted Frog

There is only one reference to a leech in the Bible, the enigmatic:

PROVERBS
CH. 30, V. 31

The leech has two daughters.
"Give! Give!" they cry.

Leeches are segmented, bloodsucking worms, of which the Medicinal Leech (*Hirudo medicinalis*) is the best known, and is found in Israel. It introduces the writer's warning that we should never feel that we are dissatisfied and need more. In the original Hebrew there is no word for 'they cry'. So the statement sounds much more dramatic if we read that the leech has two daughters, both named Give. Many people today want more and more, and are slow to offer help unless there is a positive reply to the request, 'What are you going to give me if I do it?' The jealous wants what you have, the 'Romeo' wants another girl, and the alcoholic wants another drink – which neatly lets the snake, where we began, have the last word too:

PROVERBS
CH. 23, VV. 31-32

Do not gaze at wine when it is red,
when it goes down smoothly!
In the end it bites like a snake
and poisons like a viper.

CHAPTER VII

WILD ANIMALS

We begin with a symbol of sovereignty, strength, brutality and courage, the Lion (*Panthera leo*), the second largest wild cat. Wild lions exist now only in sub-Saharan Africa and a small population in India. In the time covered by the Bible, they were widespread across North Africa and the Middle East, and were kept in menageries by the Romans.

In the scriptures we first meet a Lion when Jacob is reunited with all his sons after they had met Joseph in Egypt, and blesses them one by one with words especially chosen for each young man:

GENESIS
CH. 49, VV. 8-9

… Judah, your brothers will praise you;
Your hand will be on the neck of your enemies;
your father's sons will bow down to you.
You are a lion's cub, O Judah;
you return from the prey, my son.
Like a lion he crouches and lies down,
like a lioness – who dares to rouse him?

Judah and Joseph were given the longest blessings, which was fitting because their tribes became the leading tribes of southern and northern Israel respectively. Judah was the fourth son born to Jacob, but his three older siblings had forfeited their right to lead, so Judah was next in line and his name became the name of the whole of southern Israel in the time of the divided kingdom, roughly 900–600 BC. The Lion of Judah is still used sometimes to describe Israel today.

A striking sign of the Lion being used as a symbol of sovereignty is shown in the description of Solomon's throne at the time of the visit of the Queen of Sheba:

LION CUBS

~~ 1 KINGS
CH. 10, vv. 18-20

Then the king made a great throne inlaid with ivory and overlaid with fine gold. The throne had six steps, and its back had a rounded top. On both sides of the seat were armrests, with a lion standing beside each of them. Twelve lions stood on the six steps, one at either end of each step. Nothing like it had ever been made for any other kingdom. ~~

Solomon wanted visitors to be in no doubt about how splendid a king he was. What a difference from the way that Jesus taught his disciples to live as described in St Luke ch. 12, vv. 27–28 (see p. 75). Solomon reigned for 40 years, from 970–930 BC, and on his death the splendour of his rule was broken up and the kingdom was divided in two, Israel in the north and Judah in the south. Enmity remained between the two and neighbouring countries, till the fall of Judah in 722 BC to the Assyrians.

Travel in Palestine in ancient times was dangerous because of wild beasts. Isaiah several times speaks of the danger of being attacked by lions, but in one more hopeful comment says God will bring faithful people to a glorious, safe land:

LION

And a highway will be there;
it will be called the Way of Holiness.
The unclean will not journey on it;
it will be for those who walk in that Way;

⌇ ISAIAH
CH. 35, VV. 8-10

wicked fools will not go about on it.
No lion will be there,
nor will any ferocious beast get up on it;
they will not be found there.
Only the redeemed will walk there,
and the ransomed of the Lord will return. ⌇

In ancient times there were certain roads, such as those between temples, which were specially built to be safe. They were open only to those who were ceremonially pure. Jesus opened up the Way to everyone, when centuries later He declared to Thomas and the disciples that He was the Way. If you know Christ, you know the Way to meet God the Father; an artificial, specially designed road is not needed.

LION

The prophet Ezekiel had harsh words to say about the way the rulers of Israel had not cared for the people. Because of the pastoral lives the people led, leaders were often referred to as 'shepherds', and Ezekiel takes them to task, saying amongst other things, that:

⌇ EZEKIEL
CH. 34, VV. 4-5

You have ruled them harshly and brutally. So they were scattered because there was no shepherd, and when they were scattered they became food for all the wild animals. ⌇

Repeatedly the Old Testament writers refer to the hard, dangerous work that shepherds did. A good example is David who, before he became king, was a shepherd boy armed with a sling and stones, to protect the sheep. When he volunteered to fight Goliath, King Saul protested 'you are only a boy':

⌇ 1 SAMUEL
CH. 17, VV. 34-37

But David said to Saul, "Your servant has been keeping his father's sheep. When a lion or a bear came and carried off a sheep from the flock, I went after it, struck it, and rescued the sheep from its mouth. When it turned on me, I seized it by its hair, struck it and killed it. Your servant has killed both the lion and the bear [see p. 123] *… The Lord who delivered me from the paw of the lion and the paw of the bear will deliver me from the hand of this Philistine."* ⌇

And He did! Ezekiel and David explain very clearly how dangerous the countryside was in those days for everyone. The Psalmist wrote about it, too, in Psalm 23, with words that are often read at funerals: 'The Lord is my shepherd … your rod and staff, they comfort me'. Many years later Jesus declared that He was The Good Shepherd, which we will consider further in the next chapter.

Probably the most well known story in the Bible about lions is the tale of Daniel in the lions' den. Darius, the king of Persia appointed 120 governors to rule his kingdom, and three administrators over them. Daniel was one of the three, and soon made his colleagues jealous because of his exceptional qualities of leadership. So they tricked the king into arresting

Daniel for praying openly to God, and not worshipping the king. Darius had to obey his own law and Daniel was put in the lions' den, to be savagely executed:

At first light of dawn, the king got up and hurried to the lions' den. When he came near the den, he called to Daniel in an anguished voice, "Daniel, servant of the living God, has your God, whom you serve continually, been able to rescue you from the lions?" Daniel answered, "O king, live for ever! My God sent his angel, and he shut the mouths of the lions. They have not hurt me, because I was found innocent in his sight. Nor have I done any wrong before you, O king."

The king was overjoyed and gave orders to lift Daniel out of the den. And when Daniel was lifted from the den, no wound was found on him, because he had trusted in his God. ❧

⤳ DANIEL
CH. 6, VV. 10-23

SYRIAN BEAR

The king executed the men who had falsely accused Daniel. He prospered after that in the reigns of Darius and Cyrus, and then in the first year of the reign of Belshazzar king of Babylon he had a strange dream – which was a vision of four beasts. The first we have just read about, the lion, which later is interpreted as the kingdom of Babylonia.

Then came before me a second beast, which looked like a bear. It was raised up on one of its sides, and it had three ribs in its mouth between its teeth. It was told, "Get up and eat your fill of flesh."

DANIEL
CH. 7, VV. 3-7

After that, I looked, and there before me was another beast, one that looked like a leopard. … and it was given authority to rule.

After that, in my vision at night I looked, and there before me was a fourth beast – terrifying and frightening and powerful.

It is widely believed that Daniel was foretelling the power of the Medes and Persians (the bear), the Greeks (the Leopard) and the Romans (the terrifying beast). The bear was so well known that there is the saying 'Better to meet a bear robbed of her cubs than a fool in his folly' (Proverbs ch. 17, v. 12). The species concerned is the Syrian Bear (*Ursus syriacus*), which is regarded by other authorities as just a subspecies of the Brown Bear (*Ursus arctos*) of Europe and Asia. In Bible lands it is no longer in Israel, Lebanon and Syria, because of habitat destruction and hunting. We read of it very dramatically in one story:

2 KINGS
CH. 2, VV. 23-24

From there [Jericho] Elisha went up to Bethel. As he was walking along the road, some youths came out of the town and jeered at him. "Go on up, you baldhead!" they said. "Go on up, you baldhead!" He turned round, looked at them and called down a curse on them in the name of the Lord. Then two bears came out of the woods and mauled forty-two of the youths.

Baldness was uncommon among Jewish men, and in contrast a good head of hair was taken as a sign of strength. By insulting Elisha the youths were expressing the city's contempt for God's messenger, who was Elijah's successor and who had taken on the task of trying to bring the king of Samaria back to God-fearing ways. The bears were a symbol of the message that the whole nation would suffer if it continued to disobey God's commands. During the summer the bears live in the mountains, have a cave as a den, and feed mainly on roots and vegetables. In the winter they descend to the valleys and are known to raid gardens, so it seems most likely that this story about Elisha took place in the winter.

Daniel's other visionary animal is well attested in all translations, the Leopard (*Panthera pardus*), one of the so-called five big cats – lion, tiger, leopard, snow leopard and jaguar. It is found across Africa, the Middle East to Siberia. We can understand it was well known when we read:

JEREMIAH
CH. 13, V. 23

Can the Ethiopian change his skin
or the leopard his spots?
Neither can you do good
who are accustomed to doing evil.

The prophet was aware of the appearance of the black-skinned African and the wonderfully spotted coat of the Leopard, and expected his readers and listeners to know them too, and so understand his message to the sinful King of Israel and his people.

LEOPARD

LEOPARD

The prophet had another warning too:

> *Therefore a lion from the forest will attack them,*
> *a wolf [see p. 126] from the desert will ravage them,*
> *a leopard will lie in wait near their towns*
> *to tear to pieces any who venture out …*

⤳ JEREMIAH
CH. 5, V. 6

The prophet describes very clearly the ambushing tactic of a hunting Leopard. Notwithstanding the threat these animals posed to people, the prophet Isaiah looked forward to a time when Israel would be freed by a Messiah, a saviour, of the house of David. Then:

⤳ ISAIAH
CH. 11, VV. 6-7

> *The wolf will live with the lamb,*
> *the leopard will lie down with the goat,*
> *the calf and the lion and the yearling together,*
> *And a little child will lead them.*
> *The cow will feed with the bear,*
> *their young will lie down together,*
> *and the lion will eat straw like the ox.*

It still seems, centuries later, to be an impossible picture that these predators would ever live side by side with farm animals (see Chapter 8). But Isaiah wanted people then (and us now) to believe that the Messiah would bring that sort of peace. Christians today believe Jesus is that peace maker, and expects us to love as He loved.

Isaiah named the wolf, and from its mention there and elsewhere in the Old and New Testaments, it is clear the Eurasian Wolf (*Canis lupus*) is meant, the largest member of the dog family. We first meet it in Jacob's blessings again:

⮑ GENESIS
CH. 49, V. 27

Benjamin is a ravenous wolf;
in the morning he devours the prey,
in the evening he divides the plunder. ⮑

One can only wonder what Benjamin thought of his father's words, but suffice it to say that some of Benjamin's descendants were a fierce, savage people (see Judges chh. 19–21). The Wolf's ferocity was also referred to centuries later by Jesus when in his early preaching he told his hearers:

WOLVES ATTACKING WILD OX (SEE PAGE 137)

ST MATTHEW
CH. 7, V. 15

Watch out for false prophets. They come to you in sheep's clothing, but inwardly they are ferocious wolves. ✎

The Hebrew word for 'wolf' is *ze'ebh* and the word is even used as a man's name. One of the Midianites defeated by Gideon (Judges ch. 4) was called Zeeb, a fact recalled in Psalm 83, and the men who are the elders of Jerusalem are described as 'evening wolves, who leave nothing for the morning' (Zephaniah ch. 3, v. 3). Wolves certainly prowled around sheepfolds at night.

Wolves were clearly a very likely danger to flocks in those days and were a useful illustration for preachers and prophets. The wolf was being used as a symbol of bad ways to live, and the speakers were intent on making people aware of that, to turn them to God's good way.

Wolves are widespread across the whole northern hemisphere, and are divided into many subspecies that vary subtly in size, colour and behaviour. The form called the Arabian Wolf (*Canis lupus arabs*) is still found in southern Palestine. It is a small subspecies, mostly adapted to being a desert dweller, and weighing only about a quarter as much as a Eurasian Wolf. The species used to be the world's most widely distributed mammal, but now lives in barely two-thirds of its former range, reduced in distribution and numbers by deliberate persecution because of its preying on livestock.

There are just one or two more predatory mammals mentioned in the Bible. A teacher of the law, probably a scribe or a Pharisee, came to Jesus one day and said:

ST MATTHEW
CH. 8, V. 20

"Teacher, I will follow you wherever you go."
Jesus replied, "Foxes have holes and birds of the air have nests, but the Son of man has nowhere to lay his head." ✎

As far as we know, Jesus' enigmatic answer gets no reply from the other teacher. The man probably quickly realised that the cost of following Jesus was going to be hard; he had to be prepared to 'live rough'. The other references to foxes are all in the Old Testament and are all referred to by the same Hebrew word *shu'al* which also means 'jackal'. Is it a fox or a jackal which the Lover sings of in his song?

SONG OF SONGS
CH. 2, V. 15

Catch for us the foxes,
the little foxes
that ruin the vineyards,
our vineyards that are in bloom.

The Syrian Fox (or Jackal) is very probably the subspecies of the Golden Jackal (*Canis aureus syriacus*), which is native to the eastern Mediterranean, from Lebanon to Tripoli. It does live in a burrow, which suits Jesus' description, and is destructive in vineyards as the Lover says, because it is very fond of ripe grapes.

Isaiah in his prophecy about the destruction of Babylon wrote:

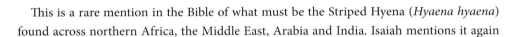

ISAIAH
CH. 13, V. 22

Hyenas will howl in her strongholds,
jackals in her luxurious palaces.

This is a rare mention in the Bible of what must be the Striped Hyena (*Hyaena hyaena*) found across northern Africa, the Middle East, Arabia and India. Isaiah mentions it again

Syrian Fox (left)

when he describes the downfall of Israel's enemies, the Edomites (Isaiah ch. 34, vv. 13–14). It is primarily a scavenger of carrion, and mainly hunts at night. Its feeding habits alone would make it a detestable creature to the Israelites, so it is an ideal animal to highlight the descriptions of desolation and death.

A very different picture of a fox is painted by Jesus when:

 ST LUKE
CH. 13, vv. 31-32

At that time [on His way to Jerusalem] *some Pharisees came to Jesus and said to him, "Leave this place and go somewhere else. Herod wants to kill you." He replied, "Go tell that fox, 'I will drive out demons and heal people today and tomorrow, and on the third day I will reach my goal.' "*

The fox clearly had a reputation then of being crafty, just as we think of it, in the story of Little Red Riding Hood, for example. Or is the word better translated as it is in this characterization?

EZEKIEL
CH. 13, v. 4
THE *GOOD NEWS BIBLE*

People of Israel. Your prophets are as useless as foxes living among the ruins of a city.

We are back to a translation problem. The *New International Version* says these prophets are 'jackals among ruins'! *The Living Bible* says 'foxes'. *The Message* prefers 'jackals'. There are foxes in Palestine, a subspecies of the Red Fox we know (*Vulpes vulpes*), or the Syrian Fox (*Vulpes thaleb*). The Hebrew word *shu'al* is used for both! It is an interesting puzzle, but whether jackal or fox, the divine message of each comment is the same – people and countries who were not going with God on life's journey were sure to suffer God's wrath, be they crafty or useless.

So much for predators. What of the prey they may have hunted? It is carefully described in the list of food that God told the Israelites they may eat, the so-called 'clean food':

DEUTERONOMY
CH. 14, vv. 4-5

These are the animals you may eat: the ox, the sheep, the goat, the deer, the gazelle, the roe deer, the wild goat, the ibex, the antelope, and the mountain sheep.

Although the commentaries admit that some of the animals and birds in the lists of clean and unclean foods are not possible to identify for certain, modern translations are in general agreement with the list above. We shall consider the farm animals in the next chapter.

So the Israelites were the hunters too, not just the wild animals! This is well attested elsewhere in the scriptures. In a warning against folly we read:

 PROVERBS
CH. 6, V. 5   *Free yourself, like a gazelle, from the hand of the hunter.*

Isaiah, too, speaks of the 'hunted gazelle' (ch. 13, v. 14). But the Beloved sees the animal very differently:

STRIPED HYENA

SONG OF SONGS
CH. 2, vv. 8-9

Listen! My Lover!
Look! Here he comes,
leaping across the mountains,
bounding over the hills.
My lover is like a gazelle or a young stag.

The gazelle is an antelope belonging to a family of even-toed ruminants, which is exactly what the law demanded – the Israelites could eat 'any animal that has a split hoof divided in two'. There are more than 20 species of gazelle, all belonging to Asia and Africa. The species still found in Palestine is the Dorcas Gazelle (*Gazella dorcas*). It stands 1.8 m (2 ft) high at the shoulders. Both sexes have horns which may be 30 cm (1 ft) long. It is an attractive animal, an ideal one to describe the Lover. The general coloration is tawny, but it is creamy white below and on the rump, and has a narrow white line from above the eye to the nostril. The Dorcas Gazelle is found singly or in small groups on the interior plains and the uplands, such as the one I saw on a ridge by the road from Jerusalem to Jericho. A herd, when alarmed, makes off with great rapidity over the roughest country, as is suggested in the description of how well one of David's men could run 'as fleet-footed as a wild gazelle' (2 Samuel ch. 2,

DORCAS GAZELLE

v. 18). The skin is used for floor coverings, pouches or shoes, and the flesh is eaten, though not highly esteemed.

The Roe Deer (*Capreolus capreolus*) is found widely across Europe and Asia. It is a little taller than the Gazelle, has a lovely red-brown hide, a white rump patch, and only the male (buck) has short, erect antlers. It is a woodland species, and in the Mediterranean region is mostly found in the hills and mountains.

The Israelites kept large herds of goats for meat and milk, and so what were the 'wild goats'?

 1 SAMUEL
CH. 24, VV. 1-2

After Saul returned from pursuing the Philistines, he was told, "David is in the Desert of En Gedi". So Saul took three thousand chosen men from all Israel to look for David and his men near the Crags of the Wild Goats.

En-Gedi means 'the Fountain of the Goat'. The Law named goat and ibex; the Hebrew word *zemer* is only used in Deuteronomy and so may be the Persian Wild Goat (*Capra aegargus*) found from the Greek islands to north-west India, and which is thought to be the ancestor of the domestic goat. Several other references, however, using the Hebrew word *yaèl*, (Job ch. 39, v. 1 and Psalm 104, v. 18) are thought to refer to the goat's relative, the Arabian Ibex (*Capra nubiana*).

The Ibex has been much hunted and is now found only as a small population in the rugged cliffs of southern Sinai where efforts are being made to protect it. Although the law says 'mountain sheep' may be eaten, the Wild Sheep or Mouflon (*Ovis orientalis*) had been domesticated by at least 9000 BC in ancient Mesopotamia. Any wild sheep that still could be found were

PERSIAN WILD GOAT

IBEX

MOUFLON

on wooded mountain slopes near the tree line in summer; in winter they came down to lower altitudes. Sheep are thought to have been one of the first animals to be domesticated and, as we have already read, Abel kept flocks in ancient times. Much more about sheep and shepherding is in Chapter 8.

Besides the list of 'clean animals', the Israelites were given a list of 'unclean animals', which they should not eat:

LEVITICUS
CH. 11, vv. 3 & 5-6

*You may eat any animal that has a split hoof completely divided and that chews the cud. …
The coney, though it chews the cud, does not have a split hoof; it is unclean for you. The rabbit, though it chews the cud, does not have a split hoof; it is unclean for you.*

The early translators did not really understand the Hebrew word *shapham* because they had no knowledge of the animal the writer of *Leviticus* was referring to – the Rock Hyrax

(*Procavia capensis*), or Coney, which is mostly a sub-Saharan species, but whose distribution spreads north through Israel to Lebanon and Syria. Furthermore, they do not chew the cud, but make a distinctive grunting sound and move their jaws at the same time, thus giving the impression to the ancient Jews that they were chewing the cud. Family groups live in underground dens in rocky territories, feed less than a 100 m (100 yd) from the entrance on plant foods, and fall prey to Leopards, snakes and eagles, if the one on watch fails to see the predator in time to sound a warning.

The same charge is levelled against the rabbit (translated as 'hare' in some versions), and repeated for both species in Deuteronomy ch. 14, v. 7. Rabbits *(Oryctolagus bicuniculus)* are not found in the Middle East – so what is really meant by the animal in the list? The Hare *(Lepus europaeus)* however, is found across Europe, the Middle East into Asia. They too move their jaws as if chewing but are not chewing the cud. Some people are upset that zoologists appear to be saying that the Bible is not true. They believe that the Word of God as written in these two quotations must be true. The writers at the time believed that what they were writing was biologically right and that God had told them to write it. The argument is discussed at length by Creationists, Hebrew scholars and modern-day zoologists. The last named have discovered that rabbits and hares pass pellets of partly digested food and then eat these pellets, a process called 'refection'. This gives them a second chance to get as much nutrition from the grass as possible. It is one part of the arguments which gives both Creationist and zoologist some comfort. As a Christian I praise God that He created rabbit

Rock Hyrax

and the hare; I respect the Jew who wants to believe his understanding of the Law; I find it most difficult to believe the Creationist's belief in the literal understanding of the scripture.

There is less to worry about with ape, monkey (or baboon), rats (or mice), wild ox, bats and fish. Ape and monkey are mentioned only once (the same statement is in two books which tell the same story):

1 KINGS
CH. 10, V. 22

&

2 CHRONICLES
CH. 9, V. 21

The king [Solomon] had a fleet of trading ships at sea along with the ships of Hiram. Once every three years it returned carrying gold, silver and ivory, and apes and baboons [monkeys in some translations].

The ape is probably the Sacred Baboon (*Papio hamadryas*). It was often painted and sculpted by the Ancient Egyptians and was sacred to their god Thoth, who was the scribe at the ritual weighing of the heart of a deceased person. They are native now to the Horn of Africa. Monkeys of several species were kept as pets in ancient times and King Solomon's were probably originally from India.

Rats and mice are mentioned in the Bible only in the list in the Law of 'unclean food':

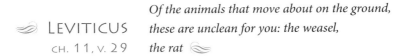

LEVITICUS
CH. 11, V. 29

Of the animals that move about on the ground, these are unclean for you: the weasel, the rat

The rest of the list names reptiles which we discussed in Chapter 6. The *New King James* translation names the first two as 'creeping things' on the earth, the mole and the mouse. There is only one member of the weasel family in our area, The Egyptian Weasel (*Mustela subpalmata*), and that is confined to north-east Egypt, so it does not seem a likely species for the Hebrews to worry about, nor does the Mole (*Talpa europaea*), which is not found around the Mediterranean. However the Palestine Mole-rat (*Spalax ehrenbergi*) is. It is a species of rodent and it does burrow like the European mole. It is a herbivore unlike the Mole whose main prey is the earthworm. It is an agricultural pest in modern Israel, storing onions and other tubers in tunnels up to 80 cm (31½ in) deep. It sends up 'mole hills' as it tunnels so would have been a noticeable pest in Bible times as it is now.

The Brown or Common Rat (*Rattus norvegicus*) is one of the commonest species of rat and is found world-wide. The Black Rat (*Rattus rattus*) originated in tropical Asia and spread to the Near East in Roman times, and is the carrier of Bubonic Plague. It is more likely that the former was known to the Israelites. The mention in the 'unclean food' list is the only Bible reference to a specific rodent.

The Wild Ox or Aurochs (*Bos primigenius*), now extinct, was the ancestor of domestic cattle (see next chapter). It ranged widely in Eurasia. Its dark colour and wide, spreading horns made it a distinctive beast. It was hunted in the Stone Age as is recorded famously in cave paintings in Lascaux, France. The animals' behaviour was well known to the Israelites too. God asked Job, "Will a wild ox work for you?" (Job ch. 39, v. 90), and more positively the Psalmist declared, 'You have made me as strong as a wild ox' (Psalm 82, v. 10).

Scholars believe cattle were domesticated over 10,500 years ago, probably from several wild species at the same time in various parts of the world. Wild cattle in the Fertile Crescent of the Near East were the likely ancestors of the cows the Hebrews kept, and are today considered to be a subspecies of the Aurochs of Europe, Asia and Africa, which survived in

BABOONS IN AN EGYPTIAN TOMB PAINTING

the wild in Europe till the mid 1600s. The Romans used them in the arena in bullfights.

There are only two references to bats. The first, oddly, is in the list in Leviticus ch. 11 of birds which are not fit to eat. The modern understanding of what is a bird as opposed to a flying mammal (which is what a bat is) was not known in Old Testament times. The Hebrew word used by the writer is *'owph* which means simply 'animal with a wing'. It was quite right to use the word for bird, bat and insect. The prophet Isaiah wrote that:

The Lord Almighty has a day in store
for all the proud and lofty
for all that is exalted
(and they will be humbled) …
In that day men will throw away
to the rodents and bats
their idols of silver and idols of gold
which they made to worship.
They will flee to caverns in the rocks
and to the overhanging crags
from dread of the Lord
and the splendour of His majesty
when He rises to shake the earth.

ISAIAH
CH. 2, VV. 12 & 20-21

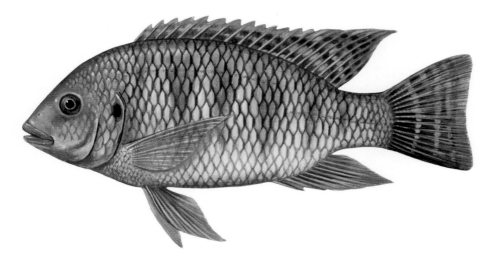

TILAPIA

The futility of idol worship and the inevitable horror of God's punishment is emphasized by the sinners having to throw their precious idols to unclean beasts. There are over 20 species of bat recorded in Israel, but we do not know from the text which ones are meant. A bat is not difficult to see at dusk, but it takes a very knowledgeable person to identify the species, and in modern times this is only possible with some species by listening to their high-pitched calls through a special monitoring device.

Fish are mentioned nearly 70 times evenly through the whole Bible. Sadly for us ,who have got used to all creatures having a name, not one species is identified, not even by King Solomon whom we are told 'taught about animals and birds, reptiles and fish' (1 Kings ch. 4, v. 33). The disciples Simon Peter and his brother Andrew were fishermen before Jesus called them and said "I will make you fishers of men" (St Matthew ch. 4, v. 19), and several stories about Jesus mention fish – for example, the boy with five loaves and two fish which miraculously fed the crowd, the amazing catch of 153 fish, and Jesus' appearance to the disciples after the Resurrection and being given a piece of broiled fish (St Matthew ch. 14, St John ch. 21 and St Luke ch. 24). The nearest we get to a name, is the popular name of St Peter's Fish being given to the commonest species caught in the Sea of Galilee. These are members of the freshwater family of *Tilapia*. The common name comes from the connection with the conversation Jesus had with Peter about taxes, because the temple tax collectors had just arrived at the house in Capernaum:

ST MATTHEW
CH. 17, VV. 25-27

"What do you think, Simon?" he asked.
"From whom do the kings of the earth collect
duty and taxes – from their sons or from others?"
"From others," Peter answered.
"Then the sons are exempt," Jesus said to him.
"But so that we may not offend them, go to the lake
and throw out your line. Take the first fish you
catch; open its mouth and you will find a four
drachma coin. Take it and give it to them for my
tax and yours."

Four drachma was the amount of annual temple tax for two men, about two days' wages each. Jesus is implying that the disciples belonged to God's royal household but disbelieving Jews did not. It is fitting that Jesus has the last word here.

CHAPTER VIII

DOMESTIC ANIMALS

Anyone familiar with the Christmas story will very quickly be aware of two domestic animals, the donkey and the camel. There are three times more references in the whole Bible to the former than to the latter. The reason is clear: donkeys were part of daily life for the many farmers and folk like Joseph and Mary as a beast of burden, whereas camels were the chosen form of transport for commercial business, carrying goods, often great distances, for far fewer merchants, or for the wealthy to ride, such as the Wise Men.

We first read of donkeys in the description of the early part of Abram's life when he travelled to Egypt to avoid the famine in Canaan. He settled and 'acquired sheep and cattle, male and female donkeys, manservants and maidservants, and camels' (Genesis ch. 12, v. 16). A family's wealth was measured in the number and quality of its livestock, so clearly Abram had become a wealthy man. Livestock were valuable, so were a legitimate spoil of war, and when Moses led the Israelites to victory over the Midianites, the soldiers took 61,000 donkeys, as well as 675,000 sheep, 72,000 cattle and 32,000 young women! (Numbers ch. 31, vv 32–33).

In Numbers ch. 22 is a splendid story about a donkey. Balaam, a pagan prophet and seer, was an expert in interpreting the future from the actions of or remains of animals – animal divination. God had forbidden him to curse the Israelites which Balak, king of the Moabites, was commanding him to do. But God does allow him to go to the Israelites, so long as Balaam follows God's instructions. He sets off intending, however, to follow his own plan and be paid a reward by Balak. He rides off on his donkey, which suddenly turns off the road down a narrow path, because it sees an angel of the Lord. Balaam beats the donkey, which says:

> ≈ NUMBERS
> CH. 22, VV. 28-30

"What have I done to you to make you beat me these three times?"
Balaam answered the donkey, "You have made a fool of me!"...
The donkey said to Balaam, "Am I not your own donkey, which you have always ridden, to this day? Have I been in the habit of doing this to you?"
"No," he said. ≈

The proverbially dumb animal was able to see the angel but Balaam, whose skills were well known abroad, was now spiritually blind. Balaam then sees the angel, and admits he has sinned. He goes to Balak and tells him at length of God's blessing of Israel. The king is very angry and sends Balaam away penniless because 'the Lord has kept you from being rewarded' (Numbers ch. 24, v. 11). Balaam's blindness is a lesson for us all, beset as we are with materialistic voices all around us.

There are several references to riding a donkey with a saddle. No doubt Mary had one for her three-day journey with Joseph from Nazareth to Bethlehem, so that they could register themselves as required for the census ordered by Caesar Augustus. That journey, and the one of well over 160 km (100 miles) shortly afterwards to Egypt to escape Herod's order to kill newborn boys, are mentioned only in St Matthew's gospel. Neither says anything about a donkey! That they travelled that way is conjecture. There is no doubt, however, about the way that Jesus rode into Jerusalem at the end of his earthly life:

DONKEY

ST MATTHEW
CH. 21, VV. 1-5

&

ZECHARIAH
CH. 9, V. 9

As they approached Jerusalem and came to Bethphage on the Mount of Olives, Jesus sent two disciples, saying to them, "Go to the village ahead of you, and at once you will find a donkey tied there, with her colt by her. Untie them and bring them to me. If anyone says anything to you, tell him that the Lord needs them, and he will send them right away."
This took place to fulfil what was spoken through the prophet:
"Say to the daughter of Zion,
'See your king comes to you,
gentle and riding on a donkey,
on a colt, the foal of a donkey'

Evidence for this donkey is in all four Gospels. The donkey had long symbolized humility, peace and royalty of the house of David – to which Jesus did belong. He deliberately rode this way to emphasize His being a peaceful saviour of the Jews, not the leader of a strong military force to oust the Romans, which is what the Zionists wanted.

The Domestic Donkey (*Equus asinus*) was bred from the wild African Ass (*Equus africanus*) about 6,000 years ago in ancient Egypt. As evidenced, for example, in Tutankhamun's tomb which has a mural depicting a wild ass hunt. The beast was well adapted for the semi-desert life of these people, and used by the early Israelites on their travels, carrying their possessions.

A trip to Palestine or North Africa today is like time travel into the past. You will see, as I have, men riding donkeys home from the fields, donkeys pulling small carts and donkeys laden with bundles of wood or animal fodder.

We assume that the Three Wise Men or Magi of the Christmas story arrived on camels. They almost certainly were well-educated astrologers from Persia or southern Arabia, so the only way in those days to travel such a long distance was by camel. They are mentioned only in St Matthew's Gospel (ch. 2), which says nothing about how they arrived, only that they came 'from the east'.

We have to read elsewhere for details about camels. The account of the Israelites' return to Jerusalem from exile in about 537 BC, is recorded in the books of Ezra and Nehemiah. There is a detailed list of the names of the people, and:

> *The whole company numbered 42,360, besides their 7,337 menservants and maidservants; and they also had 200 men and women singers*. They had 736 horses, 245 mules, 435 camels and 6,720 donkeys.*

EZRA
CH. 2, VV. 64-67

* who sang at social events such as weddings, as distinct from the temple singers who were all male

Once again we discover the huge number of livestock these people owned. Long before, Isaiah had written words of hope for the exiles saying:

> *the wealth of the seas will be brought to you,*
> *to you the riches of the nations will come.*
> *Herds of camels will cover your land,*
> *young camels of Midian and Ephah.*
> *And all from Sheba will come,*
> *bearing gold and incense*
> *and proclaiming the praise of the Lord.*

ISAIAH
CH. 60, VV. 5-6

The Midianites roamed the deserts to the east of the river Jordan and south to the east of the Gulf of Aqaba. Isaiah is referring to caravans of camels led by merchants bringing luxury goods from the east. Camels were very important because they were able to carry a considerable load and were ideally suited to barren terrain. When Joseph's jealous brothers were wondering what to do with him after they had kidnapped him:

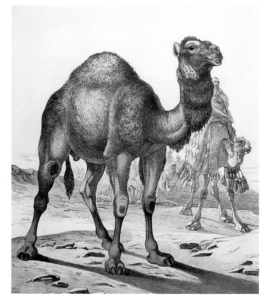

CAMEL

GENESIS
CH. 37, V. 25

As they sat down to eat their meal, they looked up and saw a caravan of Ishmaelites coming from Gilead. Their camels were loaded with spices, balm and myrrh, and they were on their way to take them down to Egypt. ⬚

These men were all descendants of Abraham, and they perfectly illustrate the length of the journeys undertaken by these caravans. Gilead was the hill country east of Jordan, between the Sea of Galilee and the Dead Sea, and their route would have been south-west via the Negev and the Wilderness of Shur, between 320 and 480 km (200 and 300 miles). Their spices are all described in Chapter 3.

These camels are the single-humped Dromedary (*Camelus dromedarius*), which was first domesticated about 4,000 years ago in Arabia. They are easier to train than cattle, so besides carrying goods, they can be used to pull a cart or a plough. An adult Dromedary can carry 160–290 kg (352–640 lb), for 24 km (15 miles) a day for a long time, thanks to its adaptation to desert life. It was an essential part of commercial transport. Camels were also valuable providers of milk, and hair, which was woven and made into clothing – 'John wore clothing made of camel's hair, with a leather belt round his waist' (St Mark ch. 1, v. 6) – and the skin was used to make a tent – St Paul stayed and worked with Aquila and his wife Priscilla when he was in Corinth, 'because he was a tentmaker as they were' (Acts ch. 18, v. 3).

Jesus named the camel in one of his talks to the disciples after He had failed to persuade a young man to give up his rich life and so find his treasure in heaven. The young man could not give up his wealth. Jesus told the disciples who were there:

ST MARK
CH. 10, VV. 23-25

"How hard it is for the rich to enter the kingdom of God!"
The disciples were amazed at his words. But Jesus said again, "Children, how hard it is to enter the kingdom of God! It is easier for a camel to go through the eye of a needle than for a rich man to enter the kingdom of God." ⬚

Jesus stresses the rich person's problem by contrasting the largest animal in Palestine with the smallest opening. Very many people today have the same problem, having a greater love of material possessions than for eternal life.

Already in Chapter 3 we discovered that agriculture was an ancient lifestyle in the Middle East, going back 10,000 years or more. Seasonal work in that era is recorded famously in the Gezer Calendar carved on stone (see p. 46). By the time of Jesus we have more documentary evidence, and it is clear that farmers were still growing crops and keeping animals as was described by Varro Reatinus (11–27 BC) in *Reum Rusticarum Libri Tres (Three Books on Agriculture)*, and by Cato the Elder (234–149 BC), author of *De Agri Cultura (On Agriculture)*, 162 chapters on home and estate management.

Animal husbandry was a continuous activity. In the beginning we read that Abel kept flocks, and these were largely sheep and goats. Sheep are believed to be one of the earliest animals to be domesticated, mostly from the wild Mouflon (*Ovis orientalis*) in Mesopotamia, for their fleece, meat and milk. Sheep were so rich a part of settled life it was only natural that the animal figures in the mythology and religion of the people of the ancient Middle East and the Mediterranean region. Shrines of the ancient Egyptians from about 8000 BC contain rams' skulls; the fertility god, Amun, was in the form of a sheep. Later, it is not surprising that we find in the Bible that sheep played an important part in the lives of Abraham, Isaac, Jacob, Moses and King David (as a boy), who were all shepherds.

Jacob and his family were suffering from famine and went to Egypt where they had heard there was still wheat. The family did not know at that time that the youngest son, Joseph, who had been sold to be a slave by his jealous brothers, was a leader in Pharaoh's court:

≈ GENESIS
CH. 47, VV. 1-3

Joseph went and told Pharaoh, "My father and brothers, with their flocks and herds and everything they own, have come from the land of Canaan and are now in Goshen." He chose five of his brothers and presented them before Pharaoh. Pharaoh said to the brothers, "What is your occupation?" "Your servants are shepherds, just as our fathers were." ≈

There was no hesitation in saying what they did, and how long the family had followed that livelihood. Throughout Old and New Testament times pastoral work was of the greatest importance, and shepherds were held in high esteem – witness the fact that shepherds were chosen to be among the first to hear about the birth of Christ:

And there were shepherds living out in the fields nearby, keeping watch over their flocks at night. An angel of the Lord appeared to them, and the glory of the Lord shone around them, and they were

≈ ST LUKE
CH. 2, vv. 9-11

terrified. But the angel said to them, "Do not be afraid. I bring you good news of great joy that will be for all people. Today in the town of David [Bethlehem] *a saviour has been born to you; he is Christ the Lord.* ≈

There are several references stating just how large the flocks were that some families had. The conquered King Mesha of Moab had to pay an annual tribute to the king of Israel of

SHEPHERDS

100,000 lambs and the wool of 100,000 rams; Job owned 7,000 sheep; and at the dedication of his temple, Solomon ordered the sacrifice of 22,000 head of cattle and 120,000 sheep and goats (2 Kings ch. 3, Job ch. 1, 2 Chronicles ch. 7). Even if these figures are exaggerated as some believe, the Psalmist praised God for His bounty by saying that the fields were covered with sheep. He must have been telling what he had seen, not just once but repeatedly (Psalm 65). There can be no doubt that sheep were a very noticeable part of daily life.

God and the leaders of Israel are symbolically called shepherds, as stated by the prophets for example:

 JEREMIAH
CH. 31, v. 10

Hear the word of the Lord, O nations;
proclaim it in distant coastlands:
he who scattered Israel will gather them
and will watch over his flock like a shepherd. ⟐

God will save his people even as a shepherd will gather together his flock after it has wandered in different directions. The image of the shepherd was used too, to warn leaders of the errors of their ways:

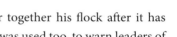 EZEKIEL
CH. 34, vv. 1-5 & 10

The word of the Lord came to me: "Son of man,
prophesy against the shepherds of Israel; prophesy
and say to them: 'This is what the Sovereign Lord
says: Woe to the shepherds of Israel who only take
care of themselves! Should not shepherds take care
of the flock? You eat the curds, clothe yourselves
with the wool and slaughter the choice animals,
but you do not take care of the flock. You have not
strengthened the weak or healed the sick or bound
up the injured. You have not brought back the
strays or searched for the lost. You have ruled them
harshly and brutally. So they were scattered
because there was no shepherd, and when they
were scattered they became food for all the wild
animals ... I am against the shepherds and will
hold them accountable for my flock. ⟐

SHEEP

This long chapter – we have here only a third of it – is a detailed account of a shepherd's work and responsibilities, and the life of the sheep. It becomes an analogy for the way all those who provide leadership – kings and their officials, and prophets and priests – and all the people they govern, should live safely and with justice together. A shepherd was indispensable. Over them all they should acknowledge that God, their Sovereign Lord, is the Great Shepherd of the Sheep. Isaiah clearly describes God as a personal, caring God, not as a remote, commanding figure (ch. 40, v. 11). This symbolical use of the sheep went seamlessly centuries later into the early Christian faith. Jesus who was brought up as a faithful Jew and well versed in the scriptures and agricultural life of his time, refers to himself as the Good Shepherd:

ST JOHN
CH. 10, vv. 14-15

I am the Good Shepherd; I know my sheep and my sheep know me – just as the Father knows me and I know the Father – and I lay down my life for the sheep.

The most striking thing about being a Palestinian shepherd was that he led the flock and they followed him, unlike an English shepherd who drives his flock, and keeps control with the help of one of more dogs. The sheep follow because they recognise the voice of their shepherd, or even the sound of the flute which some of them played.

At the end of the day the shepherd would lead his flock to the sheepfold. This was a circular area surrounded by a stone wall, open to the sky, and having only one entrance. It was well known to Jesus who used it in a figure of speech to illustrate the meaning of His saying:

ST JOHN
CH. 10, vv. 7 & 14

I am the gate for the sheep ... Whoever enters through me will be saved ... I am the good shepherd and my sheep know me.

Sheep figure in one of Jesus' most striking answers to the Pharisees who were complaining because he had healed a man on the Sabbath. Jews were not allowed to work on the Sabbath, and the Pharisees considered what Jesus had done was work. He told them:

 ST MATTHEW
CH. 12, vv. 11-12

If any of you has a sheep and it falls in a pit on the Sabbath, will you not take hold of it and lift it out? How much more valuable is a man than a sheep! Therefore it is lawful to do good on the Sabbath.

Earlier in his life his cousin, John the Baptist, had seen Him coming towards him and he told his disciples:

ST JOHN
CH. 1, v. 29

Look, the Lamb of God, who takes away the sins of the world.

This is a title for Jesus throughout the New Testament, and it comes to a climax in the last book of the Bible, in that writer's symbolic, apocalyptic style:

REVELATION
CH. 21, vv. 22-23

I did not see a temple in the city [the New Jerusalem], *because the Lord Almighty and the Lamb are its temple. The city does not need the sun or the moon to shine on it, for the glory of God gives it light, and the Lamb is its lamp.*

The imagery of shepherd and sheep is very movingly part of the later life of Simon Peter. After his denial of Christ and after the Resurrection, Peter and four other disciples were fishing when Jesus appeared and helped them bring in a very large catch of 153 fish. They all had a picnic meal of bread and fish cooked over an open fire:

 ST JOHN
CH. 21, v. 15

When they had finished eating, Jesus said to Simon Peter, "Simon, son of John, do you truly love me more than these?"
"Yes, Lord," he said, "you know that I love you."
Jesus said, "Feed my lambs."

Very significantly, Jesus questions Peter three times and to his replies says 'feed my sheep'. The message sinks home, and years later when Peter writes his first letter in the mid 60s AD to the Christians scattered in Asia Minor, he tells the elders of these churches:

1 PETER
CH. 5, VV. 2-4

Be shepherds of God's flock that is under your care, serving as overseers – not because you must, but because you are willing, as God wants you to be … eager to serve, not lording it over those entrusted to you, but being examples to the flock. And when the Chief Shepherd appears, you will receive the crown of glory that will never fade away.

Peter faithfully continued to shepherd God's flock till his martyrdom in the late 60s AD in the reign of the Emperor Nero.

Fully to understand the imagery would take another chapter! Suffice it to say that the sheep and shepherd imagery continues to this very day. Today churches across the world are led by men and women who feel they have a vocation to do this work; in English they are known by different names, depending on the denomination of the church: priest, vicar, minister, pastor – and the last title is the Latin word *pastor*, meaning 'shepherd'.

The descriptions of the wealth of the patriarchs and early heroes are strongly linked to their flocks and herds of animals. It is sometimes not easy to interpret exactly which animals are intended. In the Old Testament the Hebrew word *eleph* becomes 'cattle' in our translations. Here it is to be understood as a portmanteau term, which includes sheep, goats, oxen, donkeys and asses. In fact there are 13 different Hebrew words in the Old Testament, which are at one time or another translated as 'cattle'. In the *NIV* we often find simply 'cattle' where *Good News* expands the description to 'sheep and goats'. Translating the one term as two animals together is a reasonable interpretation because when the Israelites were in the desert for 40 years they depended on their flocks of these two animals for food and clothing. This essential wealth, which was vital to survival, is aptly recorded in the words of the writer of this proverb:

When the hay is removed and new growth appears
and the grass from the hills is gathered in,

 PROVERBS
CH. 27, VV. 25-27

the lambs will provide you with clothing,
and the goats with the price of a field.
You will have plenty of goats' milk
to feed you and your family
and to nourish your servant girls.

The milk from the goats (and sheep) was the main ingredient in the production of cheese and butter, which get just one reference each in the Old Testament. The Israelites were fighting the Philistines, and Jesse said to his son David:

 1 SAMUEL
CH. 17, V. 18

"Take along these ten cheeses to the commander of
their unit. See how your brothers are and bring
back some assurance from them."

For Jesse to have such a considerable store of cheese indicates how busy the women must have been. Cheese-making usually began in May, and goats' cheese was considered best. In such a warm climate fresh milk would soon go sour in the goat-skin bottle, so making cheese and 'churning the milk' to produce butter (Proverbs ch. 30, v. 33) were sensible things to do.

Jesus spoke about God's final judgement of everyone in a seemingly mysterious simile:

ST MATTHEW
CH. 25, VV. 31-33

When the Son of man comes in his glory, and all
the angels with him, he will sit on his throne in
heavenly glory. All nations will be gathered before
him, and he will separate the people one from
another as a shepherd separates the sheep from
the goats. He will put the sheep on the right and
the goats on his left.

In many cultures the left has been associated with misfortune, disaster, evil even. Goats were less valuable than sheep so it was natural for Jesus to put them on the left. The Romans had a word in Latin for this belief – *sinistra* – from which we get our word 'sinister'. Jesus was not denigrating the value of goats but was simply using them to illustrate the way that on Judgement Day God will separate good people from bad. But 'separating the sheep from the goats' has become an English saying to describe any two sorts of people who cannot be left together.

Notwithstanding the apparently less-than-favourable value of the goat, the animal was an important part of sacrificial worship. A man who had confessed to an unintentional sin (that is, he had done what is forbidden by God), could pay for that sin by sacrificing as a burnt offering a 'female goat without defect' (Leviticus ch. 4, v. 28).

The Domestic Goat (*Capra hircus*) is derived from the Wild Goat (*Capra aegargus*). Beginning about 10,000–11,000 years ago, Neolithic farmers in the Near East kept small herds of goats for their milk and meat, for their dung to be used for fuel, as well as for the materials they provided for clothing and building: hair, bone, skin and sinew. Archaeological evidence has revealed that domestication took place about 10,000 years ago in the valley of the River Euphrates in Turkey, and in the mountains of Iran.

It was not until the Israelites were settled in Palestine that they had pasture that was enough and suitable for rearing herds of cows. During their time in the wilderness many such animals would not have survived. But each tribe did have some cattle, as we shall read below. Herds of cattle never became as numerous as sheep and goats, but nevertheless when the people came together to celebrate the Feast of the Tabernacles and bring the Ark of the Covenant to the temple:

2 CHRONICLES
CH. 5, V. 6

King Solomon and the entire assembly of Israel that had gathered about him were before the Ark, sacrificing so many sheep and cattle that they could not be recorded or counted.

OXEN PULLING THE PLOUGH, ANCIENT EGYPTIAN TOMB PAINTING

Although 'cattle' may mean several kinds of domestic animals, clearly many cows were there. Evidence that good pasture was needed is found in the psalm praising God's bounty which says 'He makes grass grow for the cattle' (Psalm 104, v. 14). The majority of the farmers were not wealthy and may have had only one or two oxen, not to rear for beef, but as draft animals. A farmer needed to plough his land and an ox (or two yoked together) would pull the one-bladed plough, steered by the ploughman. Depending on the crops he could grow, the farmer had to plough his ground at least twice a year. The normal length of a furrow according to Varro in his book on agriculture was 37 m (120 ft), anything longer was too much of a strain for the oxen, who were rested at the turning point. They were often kept in a stall at night as recorded by the prophet Habbakuk. Oxen were also trained to pull a cart.

The law forbade a farmer from hitching an ox and a donkey together for ploughing (Deuteronomy ch. 22, v. 10), and he must not muzzle an ox when it is being used for threshing (Deuteronomy ch. 25, v. 4). The latter was carefully explained by St Paul centuries later when stating the rights of an apostle:

1 CORINTHIANS
CH. 9, vv. 4 & 9-10

Don't we have the right to food and drink? … For it is written in the Law of Moses: "Do not muzzle an ox while it is treading out the grain." Is it about the oxen that God is concerned? Surely he says this for us, doesn't he? Yes, this was written for us, because when the ploughman ploughs and the thresher threshes, they ought to do so in the hope of sharing in the harvest.

The Corinthians were being given a spiritual harvest by the apostles, so St Paul is telling them it is only fair that they give the material food and drink part of the harvest to their visitors.

Cattle were also part of the Israelites' religious ritual. The Law stated clearly that a one-year-old calf was suitable sacrifice as a sin offering (Leviticus ch. 9, v. 3). But even more demanding was the command given to Moses as they were about to escape from Egypt:

EXODUS
CH. 13, vv. 1 & 13

The Lord said to Moses, "Consecrate to me every firstborn male. The first offspring of every womb among the Israelites belongs to me, whether man or animal … All firstborn males of your livestock belong to the Lord."

God had saved every firstborn among the Israelites from death from the tenth plague, so all the firstborn were His. Jesus was presented to the Lord at the temple in accordance with this law. Firstborn animals were sacrificed (except donkeys, see below), but firstborn sons were 'redeemed', that is they were released by payment of the sacrifice of a lamb. Today we find it difficult to approve of such ritual. In fact, we probably do not think enough about sacrifice. The nearest we get to it is as I heard on the radio news as I write this – a young woman spoke of the sacrifices her parents had made to send her to university; they gave her thousands of pounds to support her study. Other people give their time volunteering to work in a hospice. Very many say they 'sacrifice' time or talent or money. But does the sacrifice hurt? The farmer must have felt some pain every time he took an animal to the altar.

Horses in the Bible are most often war-horses, pulling chariots. We first meet them in Egypt, in the Song of Moses and Miriam:

 EXODUS
CH. 15, vv. 1 & 4

I will sing to the Lord,
for he is highly exalted.
The horse and rider
he has hurled into the sea …
Pharaoh's chariots and his army
he has hurled into the sea.

When the Israelites had settled in the Promised Land, God told them that 'The king, moreover, must not acquire great numbers of horses for himself, or make the people return to Egypt to get more of them' (Deuteronomy ch. 17, v. 16), but:

2 CHRONICLES
CH. 1, vv. 14 & 16

Solomon accumulated chariots and horses; he had
fourteen hundred chariots and twelve thousand
horses, which he kept in the chariot cities and also
with him in Jerusalem … Solomon's horses were
imported from Egypt and from Kue*.

*Kue is probably the area we now call Cilicia, the south-east corner of modern Turkey.

The Old Testament is full of galloping horses, the rattle of wheels, powerful war-horses and prancing horses. But the New Testament has only three mentions of these animals.

When Paul was arrested by the Sanhedrin and was being taken for trial by Roman law (because he was a Roman citizen), the local commander:

~ ACTS OF THE APOSTLES
CH. 23, vv. 23-24

called two of his centurions and ordered them, "Get ready a detachment of two hundred soldiers, seventy horsemen and two hundred spearmen to go to Caesarea tonight. Provide mounts for Paul so that he may be taken safely to Governor Felix." ~

When James in his letter is explaining how much damage we can do by speaking, using our tongue, he says:

~ JAMES
CH. 3, vv. 3 & 8

When we put bits into the mouths of horses to make them obey us, we can turn the whole animal … but no man can tame the tongue. It is a restless evil, full of deadly poison. ~

Humans are thought to have begun to domesticate the Wild Horse (*Equus ferus*) about 4000 BC in central Asia, and scholars believe they were completely domesticated by 2000 BC, with the full range of harness we are familiar with today, as James implies. There is only one form of truly wild horse left today, the rare subspecies, Przewalski's Horse (*Equus ferus przewalskii*), of the steppes of Central Asia.

Most dramatically of all, there are the Four Horsemen of the Apocalypse. These are described in the last book of the Bible, Revelation ch. 6, vv. 1–8. The writer, St John, has a vision of Christ opening the first four of seven seals, and out come four riders, on white, red, black and pale green horses. They are the harbingers of conquest, war, famine and death, leading up to the Last Judgment. Some authorities believe the vision applied only to first-century life under the Romans. Others think a future tribulation will kill many. Yet a third interpretation sees the horsemen as representing current events, even particular beliefs, so the red horse represents Communism, the white horse Catholicism, the black horse Capitalism and the pale horse Islam. The discussion will run for a long time yet.

After those strong, large animals we finish with two small but equally important ones. Poultry is an important part of our lives for its eggs and meat, but this was not so in Old Testament times. The domestic hen is derived from the wild Junglefowl (*Gallus gallus*) of south-east Asia where it was tamed first in the Indus valley, then spread north to China and west to Egypt. There are very few Old Testament references: the 'fowl', which were a sumptuous part of Solomon's fare, may have been Pheasants or Peacocks, and not chickens, nor perhaps were they hens when Nehemiah was organizing the rebuilding of Jerusalem and 'every day one ox, six choice sheep and some poultry were prepared for me' (Nehemiah ch. 5, v. 18). It was not until Roman times that chickens were commonly kept in the west. Jesus knew them well. After His final triumphal entry into Jerusalem at Passover He spoke at length to His disciples and a crowd. The speech is sometimes called the Seven Woes, the last of which was a cry from the heart saying:

RED JUNGLEFOWL

ST MATTHEW
CH. 23, V. 37

O Jerusalem, Jerusalem, you who kill the prophets and stone those sent to you, how often have I longed to gather your children together, as a hen gathers her chicks under her wings, but you were not willing.

Jesus has just reminded his listeners of the deaths of Abel and Zechariah, which sums up the history of martyrdom in the Old Testament, and He contrasts that with His touching description, which must have been drawn from personal experience, of the way He has tried to care for people.

Even more dramatic is His conversation with Peter at the Last Supper:

ST LUKE
CH. 22, VV. 31-34

"Simon, Simon, Satan has asked to sift you as wheat. But I have prayed for you, Simon, that your faith may not fail. And when you have turned back, strengthen your brothers."
But he replied, "Lord, I am ready to go with you to prison and to death."
Jesus answered, "I tell you, Peter, before the cock crows today, you will deny three times that you know me."

Indeed, after Jesus' arrest, Peter did deny three times that he knew Jesus, as he waited outside the High Priest's house. Then he remembered Jesus' words 'and wept bitterly'. This episode in Peter's life was remembered as so important that it is recorded in all four Gospels. When compared with Peter's later life and witness for Christ, and his leadership of the young church, it is a compelling message to those first readers, and to us all now, encouraging us to believe in God's forgiveness and His grace, which can work wonders even through the actions of those who at other times have seriously failed God.

One of the keys to understanding the Bible is our comprehension of the symbolism that is hidden in the naming of God's creatures. We have read about the largest to the smallest, all with a rich tale to tell – from strength to weakness, from war to peace, from human greed to God's countless gifts of love.

FURTHER READING

Baly, Denis	1959 *The Geography of the Bible*
Beer, Endymion	2007 *Flora and Fauna of the Bible* (mostly pictures)
Bouquet, A. C.	1953 *Everyday Life in New Testament Times*
Carson, D.A. et al.	1994 4th ed. *New Bible Commentary 21st Century Edition*
Fish, Helen Dean	1998 *Animals of the Bible* (with Caldecott Medal winning illustrations by D. P. Lathrop)
Goodfellow, Peter	2013 *Birds of the Bible – a guide for Bible readers and Birdwatchers*
Hareuveni, Nogah with Frenkley, Helen	1988 2nd edition *Ecology in the Bible*
Hastings, James (editor)	1909 (1946 - 10th impression) *Dictionary of the Bible*
Heaton, E. W.	1956 *Everyday Life in Old Testament Times*
Moldenke, Harold and Moldenke, Alma	2005 *Plants of the Bible*
Porter, Richard et al.	2010 *Field Guide to the Birds of the Middle East, revised 2nd edition*
Reid, Carlton	1993 *Berlitz: Discover Israel*
Swenson, Allan A.	1995 *Plants of the Bible and How to Grow Them*
Tristram, Rev. H.B.	1884 *Fauna and Flora of Palestine*

All Bible quotations are from *The NIV Study Bible: New International Version* (1998 edition) of the International Bible Society, unless otherwise stated.

Other Bible quotations about the plants and animals studied can be found at several websites such as International Standard Bible Encyclopedia, The Jewish Virtual Library, The McClintock and Strong Biblical Cyclopedia, ChristianAnswers.net, biblestudytools.com, the Holman Bible Dictionary, or raising the name via Google.

ACKNOWLEDGEMENTS

Even as I was very grateful for help from family and friends in the writing of *Birds of the Bible*, so I am indebted now to fellow preachers Rev. Doug Rix, Roger Aldersley, Judith Allen and Kathy Brown; and to relatives and friends Heather and Stuart Norman, Hilary Farnfield, Sandie Evans and Bob Clarke, for their reading of the manuscript, and encouragement and insistence that I finish the project. I am thankful for their thoughts, which smoothed out several rough edges, and leave us with a better book.

INDEX